INTRODUCTION

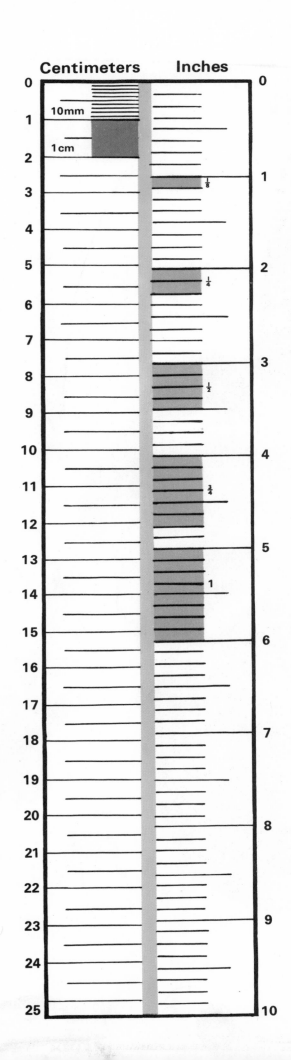

Most girls and some boys want to sew at some time or other, but how to start can be a puzzle. If you do it the wrong way you will waste your time, ruin the material and end up feeling cross.

So we have filled this book with exciting things that you will be able to make easily, if you follow the simple word and picture instructions.

There is a menagerie of stuffed animals, dolls' house furnishings, puppets, two rag dolls, clothes for them and clothes for you. And there are lots of other things besides, many of which would make excellent presents.

Full size patterns are included in the book for you to trace. Many of the items can be made out of scraps left over from your mother's sewing, or only need small pieces of material that won't cost much to buy.

Where stitches and special sewing jobs are introduced, words and pictures in blue squares show you how to do them. To look up a particular blue square, turn to the index at the back of the book, and you will find which page it is on.

Don't worry if your first efforts come out rather lop-sided; practice really does make perfect.

In some parts of the world, people use the metric system of measurement. In others, yards, feet and inches are used, and sewing materials are sold in yard lengths and inch widths.

The measurements in this book are given in yards and inches, but we thought it would be helpful if on this page we included an exact drawing of a specially designed ruler, giving centimeters and millimeters down one side and inches down the other. If you use a ruler or tape measure giving inches and centimeters, it will be easy for you to read a measurement whichever way you choose.

To test the patterns, I have been helped by some enthusiastic girls and one boy, all aged between 5 and 12 years old, who have made a remarkable collection of things from this book. My grateful thanks go to the following:

Tessa Morton   Jenny Wellington
Elizabeth Arndt   Sally Nankivell
                    Elizabeth Wegner
Hetty Wayne
                    Mark Nankivell
Caroline Arndt   Claire Morton

I should also like to thank Stefanie Harwood, my editor, for all her patient and creative help.

Janet Barber

MY LEARN TO SEW BOOK

by Janet Barber

illustrated by

Belinda Lyon

GOLDEN PRESS ● NEW YORK

Western Publishing Company, Inc.

CONTENTS

Fashion photography by Hal Jason,
model Kim Jason,
other photography by Brian Cullen.

© Copyright 1970, The Hamlyn Publishing Group Limited, England
U.S. edition published 1971 by Golden Press, New York, N.Y.
Western Publishing Company, Inc.
Printed in U.S.A.

Library of Congress Catalog Card Number: 78-148043

GOLDEN, GOLDEN NATURE GUIDE, and GOLDEN PRESS®
are trademarks of Western Publishing Company, Inc.

HELPFUL HINTS

Safety

Sewing may seem to be an activity where nothing unpleasant could happen, but accidents are possible with the sharp tools you have to use. Needles or pins, for instance, could be dangerous if they were lost in a chair or bed, or on a carpet, where they might stick into somebody's foot. When you have finished with your needles, put them into a needle-book; and your pins should go straight into a pin-cushion.

Always close your scissors when you put them down, and carry them points down. Be careful when you are using them not to cut yourself or poke them into anyone.

If you are using any electrical equipment, such as an electric sewing machine or an iron, always ask permission from your mother or a grown-up first. If you aren't quite sure how the equipment works, ask for help; and do be sure to keep your fingers out of the way of the machine needle as it goes up and down.

Cleanliness

Before you begin to sew, make certain your hands are clean. Dirty or sticky finger marks can spoil your precious material.

Sewing left lying about may pick up dust or grimy marks. If you stop for a while, always put your work into a paper or polyethylene bag, where it will keep clean.

Patience

Many items in this book can be made in one after-noon, so you will see the finished result very soon. But when you tackle the larger things, such as Polly Dolly, or some of the clothes, they are bound to take a little longer. Don't worry; take your time. Remember that sewing should give you pleasure. The moment it becomes tedious you should put it away, and come back to it when you feel in the mood to do some more.

Mistakes

Everyone makes mistakes in sewing, even people who have had years and years of practice. The best thing to do is unpick the mistake, and try again.

It is a common mistake to think that taking short cuts such as leaving out pinning and basting will get your sewing finished more quickly. In fact if you don't pin, baste and measure first, it could mean that your seams will slip and not quite match, or that a finished garment will not fit, which would be infuriating and a waste of time. Going through all the sewing stages is well worth-while.

YOUR SEWING BOX

Before you begin to make any of the lovely things in this book, you will need to collect together some sewing materials and a few simple tools. If you keep them all in a box, they will be ready for you to use whenever you feel like doing some sewing. A basket, a pretty cookie tin, or a plastic or cardboard box would be suitable, if you haven't a proper work-box.

You could begin by collecting the smaller items. Ask the grown-ups you know if they have any spares they could let you have. Otherwise you will have to spend some pocket money, and maybe drop a few hints at birthday and Christmas time!

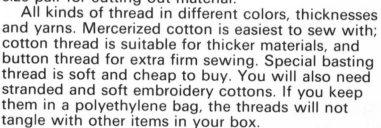

Here is a suggested list of useful things:
One small pair of scissors with sharp points for snipping thread and cutting buttonholes, and one medium size pair for cutting out material.

All kinds of thread in different colors, thicknesses and yarns. Mercerized cotton is easiest to sew with; cotton thread is suitable for thicker materials, and button thread for extra firm sewing. Special basting thread is soft and cheap to buy. You will also need stranded and soft embroidery cottons. If you keep them in a polyethylene bag, the threads will not tangle with other items in your box.

Different kinds of needles for sewing through various thicknesses of material. You could have one packet of assorted needles, a tapestry needle for canvas embroidery, a crewel needle for other kinds of embroidery and a darning needle for big stitches.

A felt needlebook, like the one opposite.

Plenty of pins. Choose the rustless kind, or glass-headed pins which are pretty and easy to use, though they cost a little more to buy.

A pincushion; you could make one yourself from the hedgehog pattern on page 12.

A safety pin or large-eyed blunt needle, for threading tape or elastic through a hem.

A small magnet to pick up pins and needles.

A close-fitting thimble for the middle finger of your sewing hand. It will save you from pricking your finger when you find it hard to push the needle through the material.

A ruler and tape measure.

Tailor's chalk or a tailor's chalk pencil, for drawing marks on material.

A soft pencil.

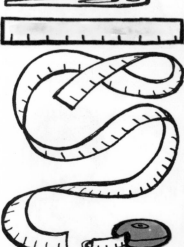

An unpicking gadget for snipping through basting stitches, and unpicking mistakes in your sewing. Use it with care, as it has a sharp point; and always put it away in its sheath.

A sewing gauge with a moveable marker—useful for checking the width of a hem as you turn it up.

Buttons cut off old garments, and spares, which you can keep in a small box.

Pinking shears for cutting a serrated edge, which stops material fraying and gives a decorative finish to raw edges. They are heavy, and not essential.

Start with something simple
SHELL SHAPE NEEDLEBOOK

**Shell shape
Cut three in felt**

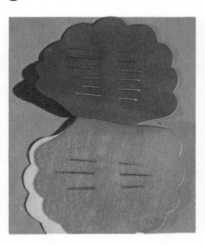

1
Lay tracing paper over shell shape pattern, and trace around outline. using felt-tip pen.

2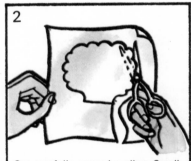
Cut carefully around outline. Small scissors are easier to use for this than big ones.

3
Lay pattern on material, close to edges. Pin about every 2 in, keeping flat, pushing pins right through pattern and material and up again.

Here is a pretty shell shape you can trace and cut out from different colored scraps of felt. This will give you good practice in making the other patterns in the MY LEARN TO SEW BOOK; and with only a few stitches you will have a useful needlebook for your sewing box.

The very youngest readers will enjoy cutting out this shape. So will the oldest, who might like to decorate it with sequins or embroidery stitches.

You will need: three 4in squares of different colored felt, or one 9in square of felt; embroidery cotton; scissors; pins; large needle; tracing paper (greaseproof paper will do); felt-tip pen.

4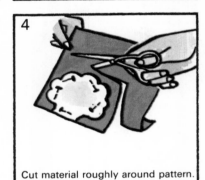
Cut material roughly around pattern.

5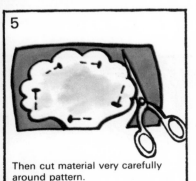
Then cut material very carefully around pattern.

6
Remove pins and pattern, and you will have your shell shape in material.

7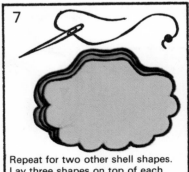
Repeat for two other shell shapes. Lay three shapes on top of each other. Cut embroidery thread, trim, dampen one end. Thread needle. Knot thread end.

8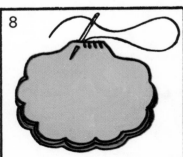
Sew shapes together along straight base of shell, with stitches that are taken through all three shapes, over and over. Cut thread, leaving short end inside.

BOOKMARKS AND BUTTERFLY BROOCH

Stitches are used for decoration, or to join pieces of material together. Here they are used to join felt shapes, and to make designs.

Bookmarks can be all shapes and sizes. Why not try designing one or two yourself?

For each bookmark, **you will need**: 9in piece of felt, or pieces to fit patterns; scraps of different colored felt; embroidery cottons; scissors; large needle; tracing paper; felt-tip pen.

For the butterfly brooch, **you will need**: a scrap of felt 2½in square; small gold safety pin; tracing materials; embroidery cotton; needle.

Pepper mill

Running stitch

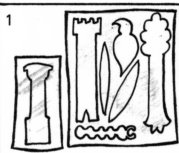

1 Trace outlines of patterns, drawing eyes, feathers, orange and lemon shapes separately, and cut out.

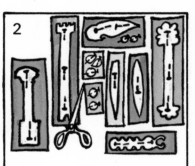

2 Pin patterns to felt and cut out shapes. When you have cut them out, remove pins and patterns.

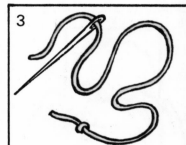

3 Thread needle, and tie knot in end of embroidery thread—not too long or it may tangle.

4 Copy running stitch designs on to felt shapes, as shown in pictures.

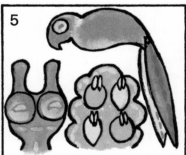

5 Stitch oranges and lemons to tree, eye and tail to parakeet, and eyes to bookworm.

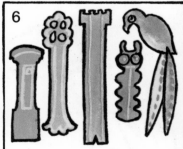

6 Bookmarks make good presents.

1 Thread needle and make knot near end of thread. Working from right to left, push needle from back of material through to front.

2 Keep needle level, and push it in and out of material, making stitches and spaces equal.

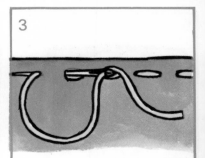

3 To finish off, go back to end of last stitch and bring needle through again. Repeat. Cut off thread at back not too close to material.

10

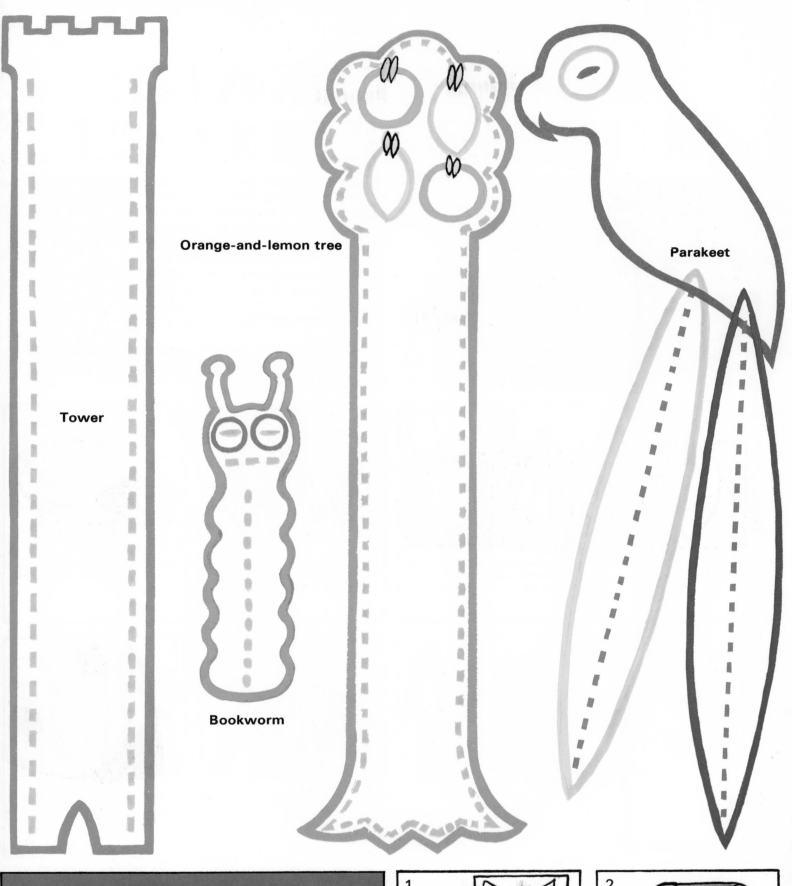

Tower

Orange-and-lemon tree

Bookworm

Parakeet

Butterfly brooch

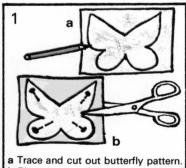

1

a Trace and cut out butterfly pattern.
b Pin pattern to felt and cut out one butterfly shape.

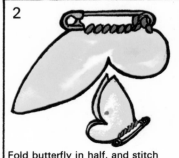

2

Fold butterfly in half, and stitch along back of gold safety pin.

HEDGEHOG PINCUSHION

What could be friendlier than this hedgehog pincushion, sitting by you as you sew, his pin prickles ready for you to borrow whenever you need them!

Some pincushions are large and stand on the table. Another kind is small, round and plump, with a bracelet of elastic stitched on the back. You wear it on your wrist while you work. Soft materials such as felt, velvet or corduroy are best to use.

You will need: two pieces of different colored felt, each 5in by 3½in; black and colored embroidery cotton; stuffing (kapok or cotton wool); scissors; glass-headed pins; large needle; tracing paper; felt-tip pen.

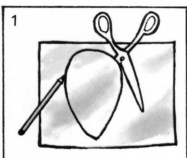

1 Trace outline of hedgehog and cut out paper pattern.

2 Pin pattern to felt and cut out shape. Repeat with second piece of felt.

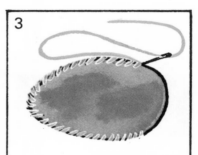

3 Place both shapes together. Oversew around edge, leaving opening for stuffing.

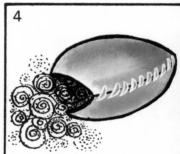

4 Push stuffing through opening, making hedgehog as fat as possible.

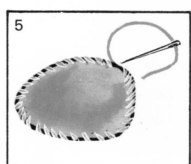

5 Press edges of opening together and oversew neatly.

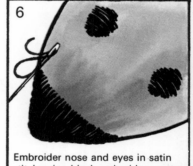

6 Embroider nose and eyes in satin stitch using black embroidery cotton.

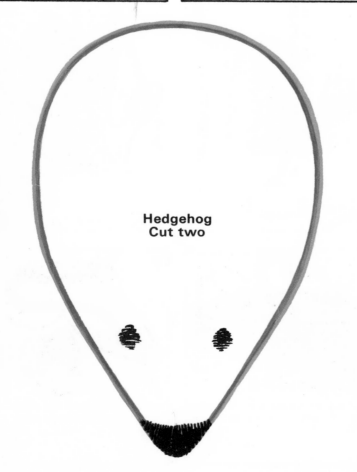

Hedgehog Cut two

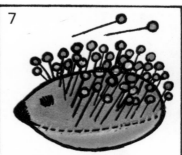

7 Stick the pins in for prickles—not too far, or they may poke through underneath.

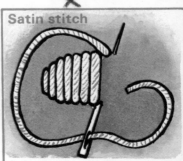

Satin stitch

Satin stitch is rather like oversewing. The stitches go over and over, but are very close together. They may be slanted, if you prefer.

FINGER FAMILY

This family of finger puppets can be fitted on to your fingers, some on each hand, and then you can act with them. If you kneel behind a table and put your hands against the edge with the puppets showing above, you can make them walk and dance and have funny conversations. You could add your own characters: a cat, a granny, and so on.

If you want the finger puppets to stand up by themselves, push some cotton wool inside them. Made like this they can stand inside your dolls' house to give it a family of its own.

You will need: scraps of felt; embroidery cotton; scissors; large needle; paper; pencil.

1 Place hand on paper and draw around each finger down to knuckle, allowing ¼in extra all around.

2 Cut out paper patterns. Pin to felt, and cut out two shapes for each puppet.

3 Cut out a round face for each "person". Sew on to front shape with stitches which make eyes and mouth.

4 Oversew front shape to back shape, leaving opening for finger.

5 Give Pa a moustache and wide tie. Ma has an apron sewn on with running stitch.

6 Sam has a scarf, and Pam braids with bows. Hair is oversewn, but leave ends for Pam's braids.

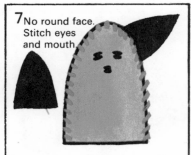

7 No round face. Stitch eyes and mouth. Cut out two black felt ears for Fred Dog, and stitch them on.

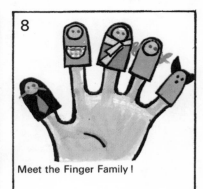

8 Meet the Finger Family!

Oversewing

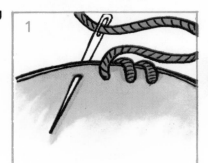

1 Work from right to left. Knot thread, and bring needle through from back of material just under edge. Pull thread through. Repeat.

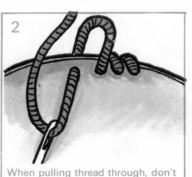

2 When pulling thread through, don't pull too tight or material will pucker.

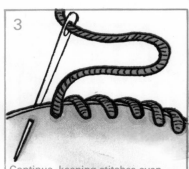

3 Continue, keeping stitches even. This is a good stitch to use to stop a raw edge from fraying, to close a gap, or to join pieces of felt together.

INSIDE YOUR DOLLS' HOUSE

If you would like to make a simple dolls' house, stand a cardboard box on its side, and glue another on top to make an upstairs. The windows could be cut out or painted on, and the walls papered with wall-paper, or little pin-ups cut out from magazines. Contact plastic makes good floor covering.

For pictures, use small photographs, pretty postage stamps, or your own tiny paintings and drawings. You can make a bed by gluing one match box cover beside another, and adding a cardboard bedhead. The table in the picture is made from a piece of cardboard for the top (draw around a jar), glued on to a covered cotton reel. When the house is complete, paint it outside.

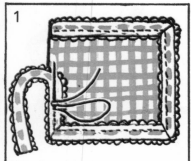

1 To make **bedcover**, measure your dolls' house bed and cut out felt to fit.

2 Lay pompon trimming flat over edge of felt and sew on with running stitch.

3 To make **bolster**, cut felt 3in long to fit across bed. Running stitch down both sides. Shape into tube and stitch edges together.

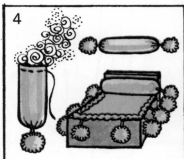

4 Gather one end tightly, and sew on pompon trimming. Stuff. Repeat at other end.

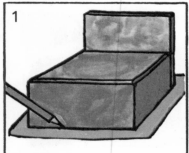

1 To make **lamp** and **lampshade**, cut felt to fit around cotton reel. Sew lace flower on front or embroider. Make into tube, sew down side, and slip on reel. Cut felt disc for top.

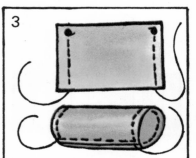

2 Gather top of lace strip with running stitch. Pull thread tight, and tie in bow. Push pencil stub into cotton reel, and put lampshade on it.

1 To make **tablecloth**, cut square to fit dolls' house table. Sew ribbon flat around edges with running stitch.

2 **Curtains**. Cut out and gather along top to fit dolls' house window. Sew ribbon along lower edge. Pin across window under ribbon valance with drawing pins.

You will need: cotton reels; pipe cleaners; matchboxes; scraps of felt and different materials; pieces of lace; fringe and pompon trimming; ribbon; scissors; pins; needles; embroidery cotton; thread; wool; stuffing; pencil stub; toothpaste cap; cardboard; glue; drawing pins; pencil; ruler.

Bench seat, cushions and floor pillow

1 Cut out strip of felt to cover outside of matchbox. Fold to fit, join ends with running stitch, and slip over box.

2 For cushion, cut out a strip of felt same width. Fold up to form a bag and sew up sides. Stuff.

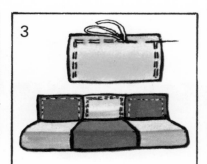

3 Sew across top opening, and place above seat. Three, side by side, make a sofa.

4 To make floor pillow, draw around jar on felt. Cut two shapes, join with running stitch, leaving opening. Stuff, and sew up opening. Sew stitch through center.

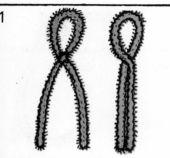

1 **Pipe-cleaner people.** Wind two pipe cleaners into these shapes.

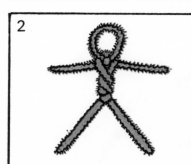

2 Pass ends of red one through loop of green one. Bend red ends out for arms, cut shorter and press sides of green loop together.

3 Wind wool around pipe cleaners, up and down several times. Embroider mouth and eyes, and oversew hair.

4 To make dress, wrap strip of felt around doll, cut, and stitch up side. Make children from pipe cleaners cut shorter.

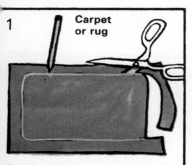

1 **Carpet or rug** Decide what size you want it to be. Draw shape on to felt, and cut out.

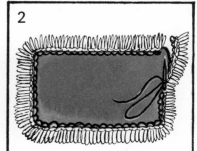

2 Lay fringe braid flat on edge and sew on with running stitch.

The rubber tree plant is made from a pipe cleaner, with felt leaves stitched on, pushed into a covered cotton reel. A pot of flowers can be made of two felt flowers and two felt leaves, all very small, stitched to a 2 in pipe-cleaner bent in half, to fit into the cap of a toothpaste tube.

You could also make a small towel and bath mat for the bathroom. Make a towel ring by cutting 1½ inches of narrow tape, passing it through a curtain ring, and fixing it to the wall with a drawing pin.

Don't forget the garden! A green felt lawn, with colored felt flowers sewn on pipe cleaner stalks, stuck in modeling clay, would look pretty.

HEN EGG COSY

When you start learning to sew, you will soon want to join different shapes together.

Shapes are joined by sewing a line of stitches through two layers of material, which makes a seam. There are many different kinds of seams; the one on this page is a plain seam sewn in back stitch, but you could use running stitch. The distance between the seam and the edge of the material is called the seam allowance; here, it is $\frac{1}{4}$in.

You will need: 9in square of brown felt; scraps of dark brown felt for wings and eyes; embroidery cotton in yellow and blue; scissors; pins; large needle; tracing paper; felt-tip pen.

1
Trace outline of hen, wing and eye, and cut out patterns.

2
Pin patterns to felt, and cut out two of each.

3
Sew eyes and wings on to sides of hen.

4
To join the two shapes together, pin, baste and back stitch all around, except along the lower edge. Remove basting.

5
Blanket stitch along lower edge.

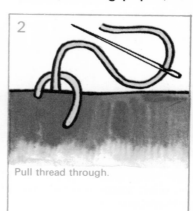

1 Blanket stitch

Work from left to right with thread at top edge. Point needle upwards, push through material from front to back, and bring out between material and thread.

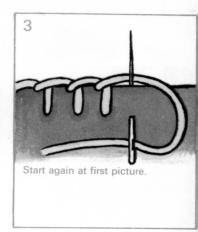

2

Pull thread through.

3

Start again at first picture.

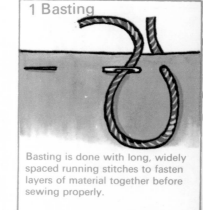

1 Basting

Basting is done with long, widely spaced running stitches to fasten layers of material together before sewing properly.

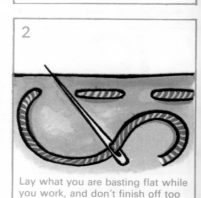

2

Lay what you are basting flat while you work, and don't finish off too tightly as the basting threads are pulled out later.

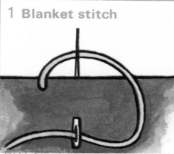

GHOST GLOVE PUPPET

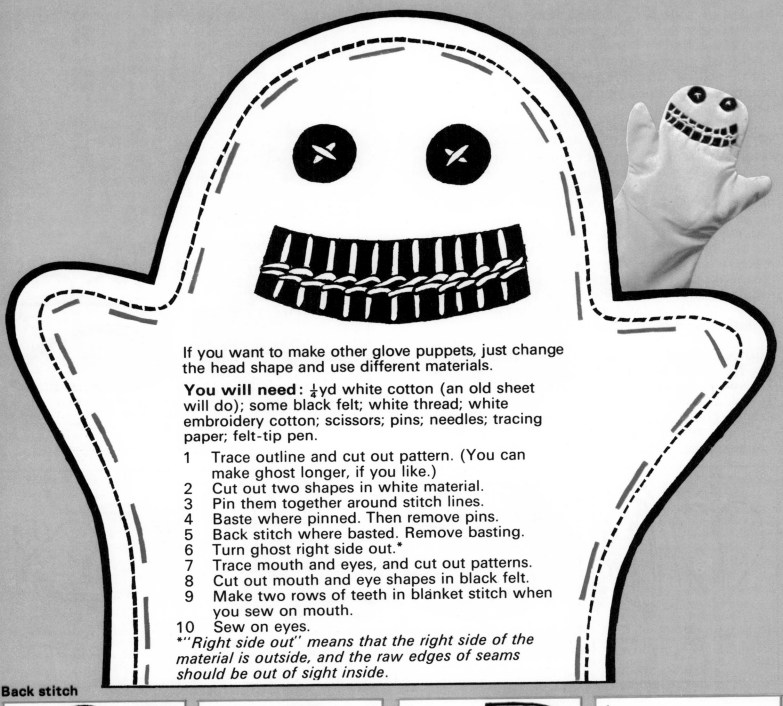

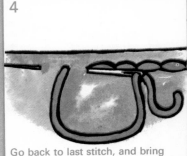

If you want to make other glove puppets, just change the head shape and use different materials.

You will need : $\frac{1}{4}$yd white cotton (an old sheet will do); some black felt; white thread; white embroidery cotton; scissors; pins; needles; tracing paper; felt-tip pen.

1 Trace outline and cut out pattern. (You can make ghost longer, if you like.)
2 Cut out two shapes in white material.
3 Pin them together around stitch lines.
4 Baste where pinned. Then remove pins.
5 Back stitch where basted. Remove basting.
6 Turn ghost right side out.*
7 Trace mouth and eyes, and cut out patterns.
8 Cut out mouth and eye shapes in black felt.
9 Make two rows of teeth in blanket stitch when you sew on mouth.
10 Sew on eyes.

*''Right side out'' means that the right side of the material is outside, and the raw edges of seams should be out of sight inside.

Back stitch

Working from right to left, start with a knot at the back. Bring needle through to front and then go back the length of one stitch.

Push needle in, pass it under material, and bring it out the length of a stitch in front.

Draw needle and thread out.

Go back to last stitch, and bring needle forward under material as in square 2. Repeat from square 3.

Stuffed animals and toys
MOUSE

Stuffed toys are easy and quick to make, if you follow the step - by - step instructions carefully.

You will find that they can be inexpensive to make if you use pieces of material, and stuff them with cut up scraps. But if you prefer to use new material, we have given the amounts you will need to buy for each one.

As this delightful mouse is so simple to sew, why not make some more in different colors to keep him company on your shelf? You could give him a wife, and some baby mice cut the same way, but smaller. Join tiny mice on the outside with running stitch seams.

Sewing instructions sometimes say "right sides facing" or "wrong sides facing" when pieces of material are placed together. "Right sides facing" means that you match the right sides of material together, with wrong sides out. "Wrong sides facing" means that the wrong sides of material are matched together, with right sides out.

You will need : 9 in square of felt; or a scrap of felt 4 in by 5 in for sides, and another scrap of felt 4 in by 2 in for underside; scraps of felt for ears; thread; stuffing (cotton wool or kapok); black stranded cotton for eyes, nose and claws; wool or colored soft embroidery cotton for tail; scissors; needles; pins; tracing paper; felt-tip pen.

1

Trace and cut out patterns. Pin to felt and cut out shapes: two sides, one underside, two ears.

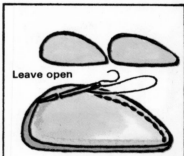

Leave open

Pin sides together. Back stitch around top, leaving tail end and lower edge open. Remove pins.

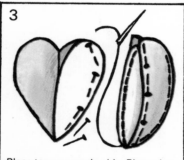

3

Place top over underside. Pin underside to lower edges of top, leaving tail end open for stuffing. Back stitch around.

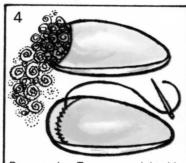

4

Remove pins. Turn mouse right side out and stuff. Oversew neatly along opening.

5

Pleat ears, and oversew on to head. Thread needle with wool or embroidery cotton and sew on for tail.

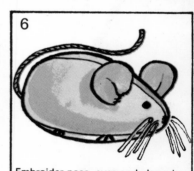

6

Embroider nose, eyes and claws in black. Cut lengths of white thread, fold in half, and stitch to face for whiskers.

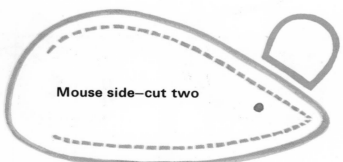

Mouse side—cut two

Ear
Cut two

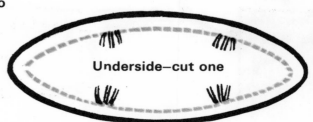

Underside—cut one

FLOPPY FROG

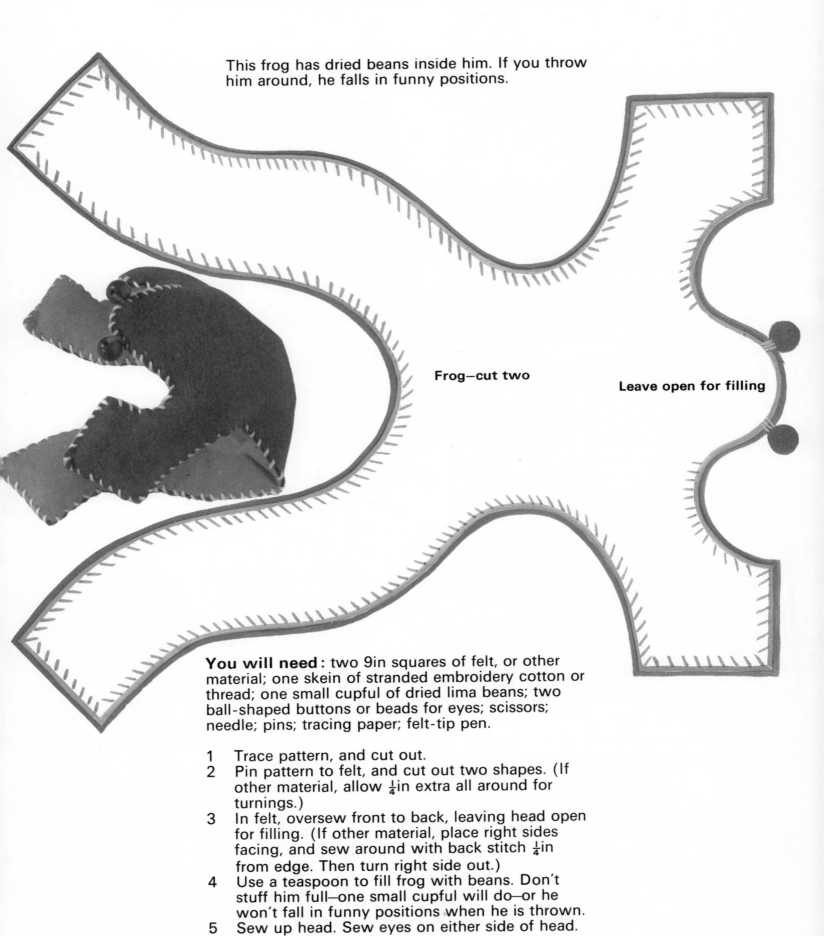

This frog has dried beans inside him. If you throw him around, he falls in funny positions.

Frog—cut two

Leave open for filling

You will need: two 9in squares of felt, or other material; one skein of stranded embroidery cotton or thread; one small cupful of dried lima beans; two ball-shaped buttons or beads for eyes; scissors; needle; pins; tracing paper; felt-tip pen.

1 Trace pattern, and cut out.
2 Pin pattern to felt, and cut out two shapes. (If other material, allow $\frac{1}{4}$in extra all around for turnings.)
3 In felt, oversew front to back, leaving head open for filling. (If other material, place right sides facing, and sew around with back stitch $\frac{1}{4}$in from edge. Then turn right side out.)
4 Use a teaspoon to fill frog with beans. Don't stuff him full—one small cupful will do—or he won't fall in funny positions when he is thrown.
5 Sew up head. Sew eyes on either side of head.

You can fill your frog with rice grains, but the stitches must be very small and close together.

LAZY-DAISY CAT

Here is a three-cornered cat. He is made of velvet, and embroidered with lazy-daisies.

Velvet has fur, like a cat. The furry side is called the pile. You can stroke it more easily one way than the other. When you cut out patterns in velvet, always make sure the pile is going in the right direction by stroking it, and seeing which way it lies. Otherwise it will look wrong when you make it up.

You will need : ¼yd velvet; scraps of felt for eyes and ears; thread; soft or stranded embroidery cotton in three colors; stuffing (kapok, foam plastic chippings or old nylons cut up); scissors; pins; a large and a small needle; tracing paper; felt-tip pen.

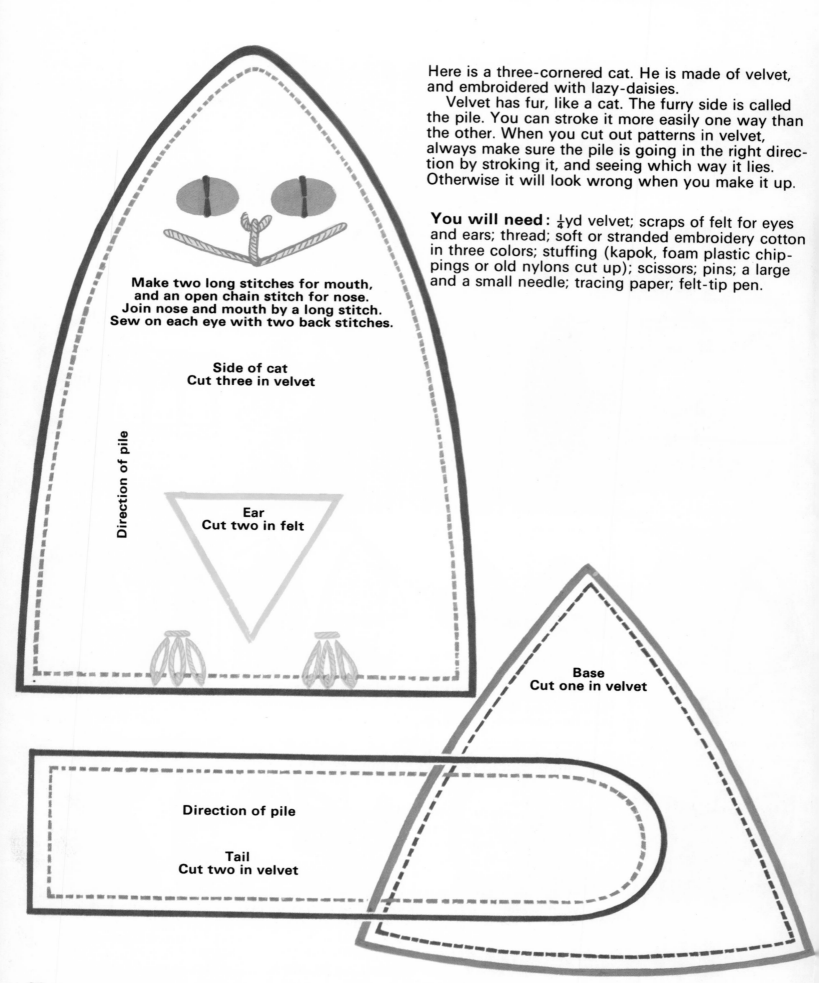

Make two long stitches for mouth, and an open chain stitch for nose. Join nose and mouth by a long stitch. Sew on each eye with two back stitches.

Side of cat
Cut three in velvet

Direction of pile

Ear
Cut two in felt

Base
Cut one in velvet

Direction of pile

Tail
Cut two in velvet

1

Trace and cut out patterns, including separate eyes and ears.

2
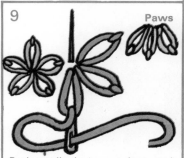
Pin patterns to material and cut out shapes. Remember to keep velvet pile going same way for all three sides of cat.

3
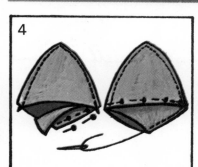
Pin, baste, then back stitch three sides together, one at a time, working from bottom to top, pile side inward. Join **1** to **2**, **2** to **3**, then **3** to **1**.

4

Right sides facing, pin sides of base triangle to lower edges of sides, leaving one open for stuffing. Baste, back stitch, and remove pins.

5
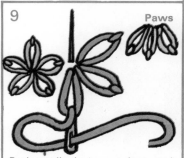
Turn right side out and stuff. Turn in and sew up opening.

6

Right sides facing, pin, baste and back stitch tail shapes together, leaving top open for stuffing. Turn right side out, stuff, turn in and sew to body.

7
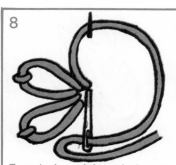
Pleat and sew ears to head along seams at side of face. Sew on eyes. Embroider mouth and nose, and make whiskers as on mouse.

8
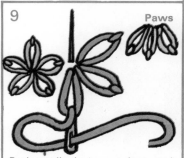
To make **lazy-daisy stitch**, push needle in at center of daisy, and bring out at petal tip, thread looped behind needle.

9
Paws

Push needle down, over loop, and bring up again where next petal starts—at center, if you are making complete daisy.

10
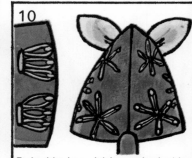
Embroider lazy-daisies on both sides of cat's back, and lazy-daisy paws of 3 petals each, side by side, at lower front edge.

BEAN BAG SNAKE

You can make this wriggly snake twice as long by retracing the body below the neck, and pinning the second pattern just above the tail on the first pattern.

You will need: $\frac{1}{8}$ yd material for the pattern on this page, or $\frac{1}{4}$ yd if you make it longer (Make the top a different color from the underside, if you like; felt, cotton and whipcord are good); scraps of felt for eyes and forked tongue; thread; soft embroidery cotton; dried lima beans for filling; scissors; pins; needle; tracing paper; felt-tip pen.

1 Trace outline of snake, eyes and tongue, and cut out separate patterns.
2 Cut out two snake shapes, two eyes and one tongue.
3 Right sides facing, pin and baste top to underside of snake. Remove pins.
4 Back stitch all around except for mouth end, which is left open for filling. Remove basting.
5 Turn snake right side out, and fill with beans. Turn in opening and oversew.
6 Sew on tongue under head, and eyes on head with two back stitches each.
7 Embroider zig-zag line down back in chain stitch.

Chain stitch

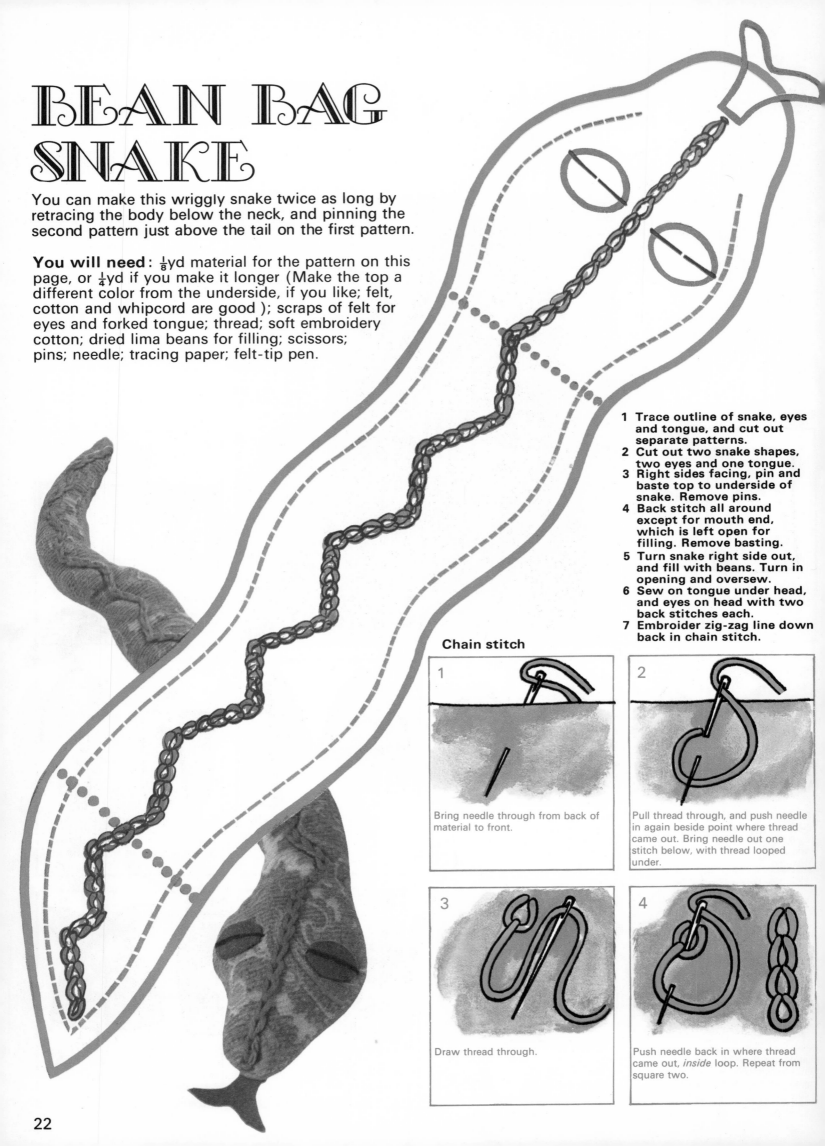

1 Bring needle through from back of material to front.

2 Pull thread through, and push needle in again beside point where thread came out. Bring needle out one stitch below, with thread looped under.

3 Draw thread through.

4 Push needle back in where thread came out, *inside* loop. Repeat from square two.

HUMPERS DUMPERS

Sew front to back around this line

Sew hand here

Sew hand here

Sew trousers on here, then braid

Humpers Dumpers
Cut two

You will need: material 6in by 10in for Humpers Dumpers' body; material 4in by 10in for trousers; scraps of felt for feet, hands and face; thread; stuffing; 9in braid for cummerbund; wool for hair; cardboard and stranded cotton for guitar; scissors; pins; needle; glue; tracing paper; felt-tip pen.

1 Trace and cut out patterns.
2 Pin patterns to material and cut shapes, placing trouser pattern on fold. Cut trouser fold away where shown.
3 Right sides facing, back stitch front of body to back, leaving opening for stuffing.
4 Turn right side out, stuff, and sew up opening.
5 Sew on hands where shown, and feet inside back of trousers.
6 Wrap trousers around Humpers, matching center fold to center back, and stitch around waist.
7 Sew front to back of trousers between legs with running stitch. (Match A to B).
8 Sew braid around trousers with running stitch.
9 Sew wool on head for hair, and cut to look shaggy.
10 Cut out eyes, nose and mouth. Attach to face with running stitch or glue.

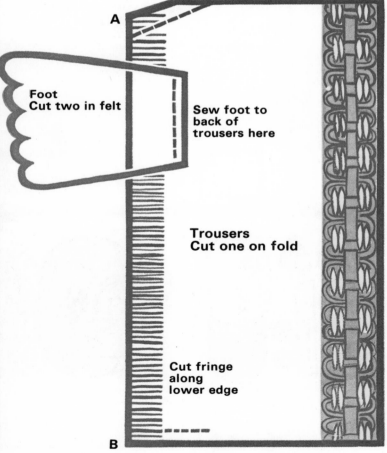

A

Foot
Cut two in felt

Sew foot to back of trousers here

Trousers
Cut one on fold

Cut fringe along lower edge

B

Hand
Cut two in felt

To make guitar:
Draw a guitar shape on to a piece of cardboard measuring 5in by 1¾in, and cut out. Take a small button and draw a circle on the guitar shape for the hole in the soundbox. Paint the guitar bright yellow, or your own choice of color, and the circle another color.

Using embroidery cotton, make two long stitches through the cardboard from end to end of the guitar for strings, and one long loose stitch at the back to hang the guitar around Humpers Dumpers.

ELEPHANT CUSHION

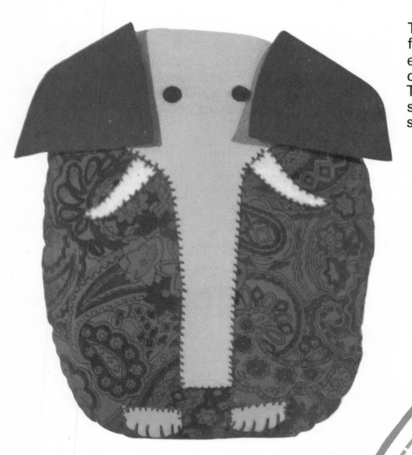

This elephant's face is made of different material from its body, and is sewn on top, all around the edge. Sewing different fabrics flat on top of each other like this, to make a design, is called appliqué. The appliqué shapes here are sewn on with hemming stitch, but you can use other stitches, such as running stitch or blanket stitch.

Cushion shape
Cut one front
in patterned material,
and one back
in felt, on fold

Foot
Cut two

Leave open
for stuffing

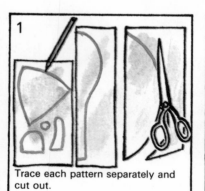

1 Trace each pattern separately and cut out.

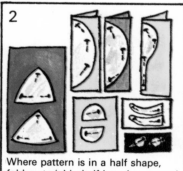
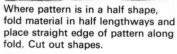

2 Where pattern is in a half shape, fold material in half lengthways and place straight edge of pattern along fold. Cut out shapes.

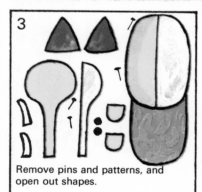

3 Remove pins and patterns, and open out shapes.

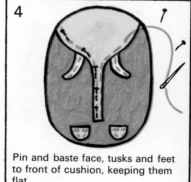

4 Pin and baste face, tusks and feet to front of cushion, keeping them flat.

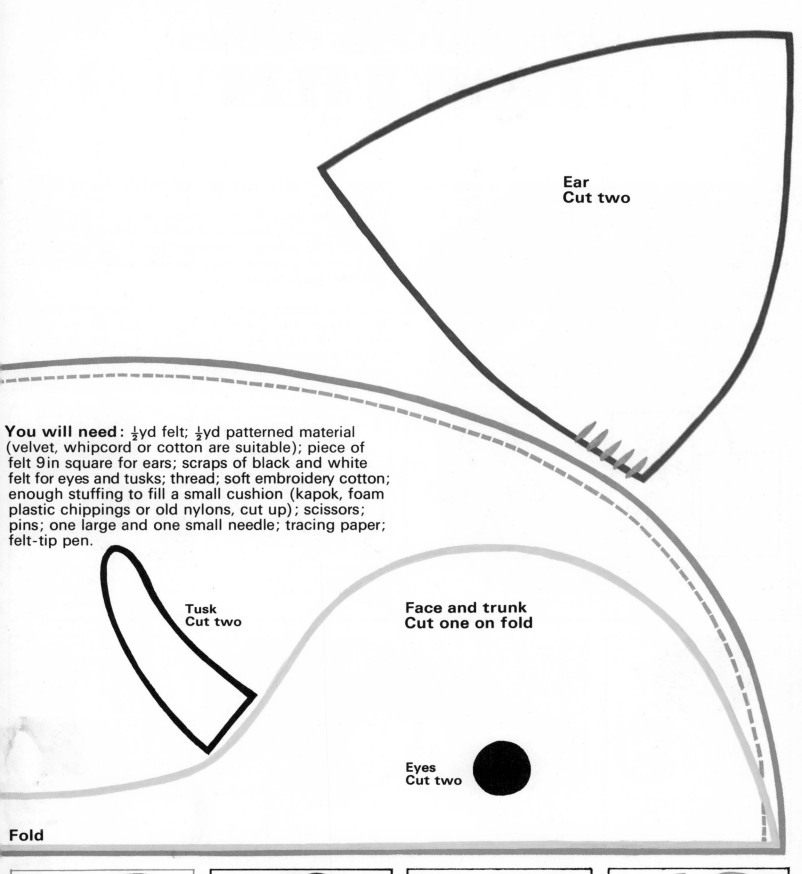

**Ear
Cut two**

You will need: ½yd felt; ½yd patterned material (velvet, whipcord or cotton are suitable); piece of felt 9in square for ears; scraps of black and white felt for eyes and tusks; thread; soft embroidery cotton; enough stuffing to fill a small cushion (kapok, foam plastic chippings or old nylons, cut up); scissors; pins; one large and one small needle; tracing paper; felt-tip pen.

**Tusk
Cut two**

**Face and trunk
Cut one on fold**

**Eyes
Cut two**

Fold

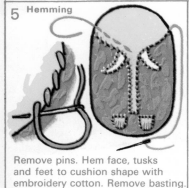

5 Hemming

Remove pins. Hem face, tusks and feet to cushion shape with embroidery cotton. Remove basting. Blanket stitch toes.

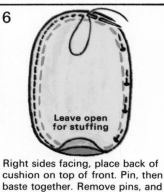

6

Leave open for stuffing

Right sides facing, place back of cushion on top of front. Pin, then baste together. Remove pins, and back stitch all around, leaving opening for stuffing.

7

Turn right side out, and stuff through opening until firm. Turn in edges of opening, and oversew neatly to close.

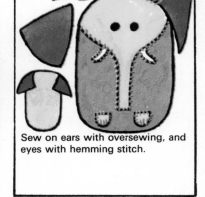

8

Sew on ears with oversewing, and eyes with hemming stitch.

Dolls and dolls' clothes
BABY BILLY

Here are two rag dolls for you to make: a little one called Baby Billy, and his big sister, Polly Dolly. The clothes for you to dress them in come on the following pages.

It takes a little longer to make Polly Dolly than Baby Billy, who is cut out all in one piece, but you will be so proud of having your own family of dressed dolls that it will be worth making them both.

As you make them up, step by step, you will be amazed to find how much you are learning about sewing—without even noticing !

When you've completed them, you may like to give them each a cardboard box bed and some bed clothes. Have a look at the picture of Baby Billy tucked up in bed; perhaps you would like to make one like it.

To make Baby Billy a diaper, cut out a 5in square of toweling or other soft material—even paper tissue will do. Place diaper between legs, bring up at front and back, and fasten back corners over front corners with two gold safety pins.

You will need : $\frac{5}{8}$yd calico or other material for doll; thread; 1oz skein of wool for hair; blue and bright pink embroidery thread for face; kapok, foam plastic chippings, or old nylons, cut up, for stuffing; scissors; pins; needles; pencil; thick plastic knitting needle to push in stuffing; tracing paper; felt-tip pen.

1 Trace and cut out pattern. Pin to material and cut out shape. Repeat for second shape.

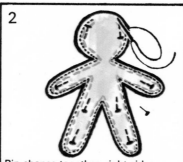

2 Pin shapes together, right sides facing. Baste. Remove pins. Back stitch around, leaving top of head open for stuffing.

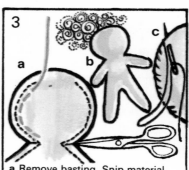

3 a Remove basting. Snip material where shown on pattern. **b** Turn right side out and stuff. **c** Sew up opening.

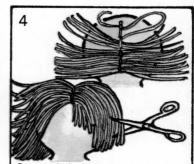

4 Sew on hair, four strands at a time, using back stitch. Start at back and work up. Sew on more strands to make fringe, with stitches going across head. Trim.

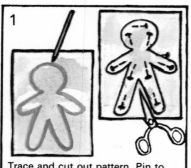

5 Draw Billy's face on with pencil. Embroider blanket stitch eyes, joining ends of stitches at center, like wheels.

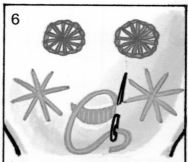

6 Satin stitch mouth. For star cheeks, use one strand embroidery cotton and cross four stitches over each other.

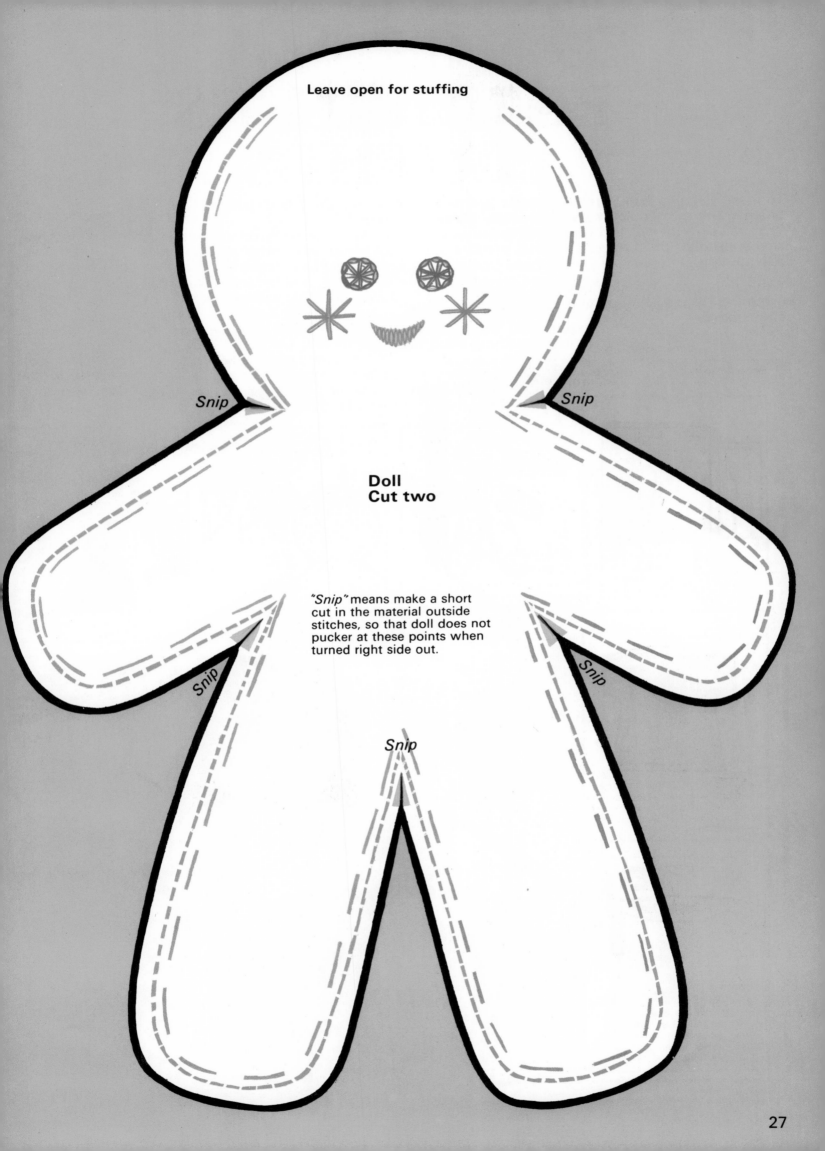

Leave open for stuffing

Snip

Snip

**Doll
Cut two**

"Snip" means make a short
cut in the material outside
stitches, so that doll does not
pucker at these points when
turned right side out.

Snip

Snip

Snip

BABY BILLY'S CLOTHES

To make sleeping bag **you will need**: $\frac{1}{4}$yd brushed orlon or similar material (a piece 9in by 18in will do); thread; 1yd bias binding; two snaps; needles; pins; scissors; tracing paper; felt-tip pen.

You can also make a nightgown in flannelette, using the sleeping bag pattern, but leaving the lower edge open.

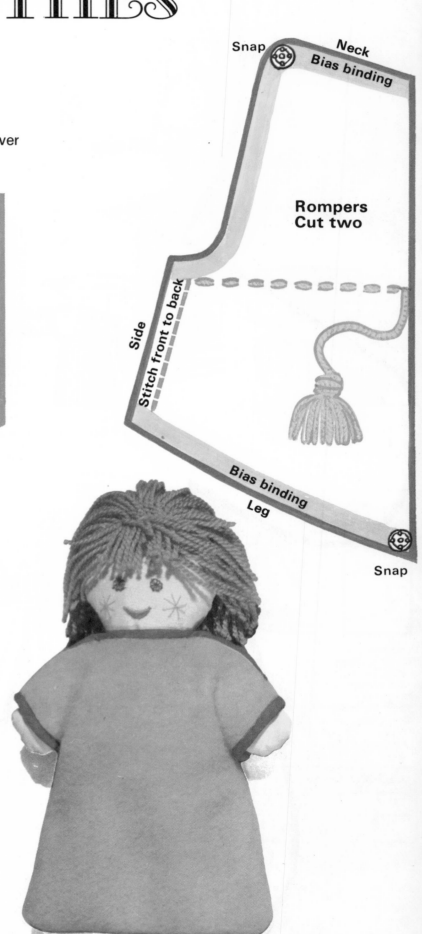

Rompers
Cut two

Snap · Neck
Bias binding

Side · Stitch front to back · Bias binding · Leg · Snap

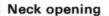

Neck opening

Bias binding · Snap · **Shoulder**

Bias binding · Arm hole

Sleeping bag
Cut two

Fold

Stitch front to back along this line

Lower edge

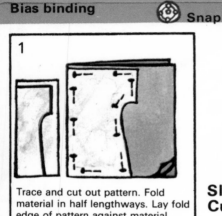

1

Trace and cut out pattern. Fold material in half lengthways. Lay fold edge of pattern against material fold. Cut out shape. Repeat for second shape.

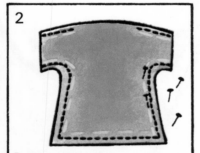

2

Remove pattern. Open out shapes. Pin, then baste together, right sides facing. Remove pins. Join with back stitch, where shown on pattern. Remove basting.

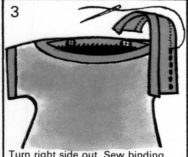

3

Turn right side out. Sew binding along front and back of neck and around sleeves, turn in ends, and stitch down to neaten. Sew a snap at each side of neck.

28

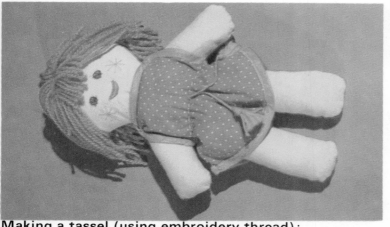

To make rompers, **you will need**: $\frac{1}{4}$yd cotton or flannelette (a piece 12in by 6in will do); thread; 1yd bias binding; 1 skein embroidery cotton; 3 snaps; scissors; needles; pins; tracing paper; felt-tip pen.

Making a tassel (using embroidery thread):

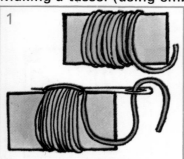

1 Cut out card and wind cotton around it. Pass threaded needle under top of tassel twice and tie in knot.

2 Cut tassel through at lower edge Wind cotton around below top of tassel and finish off at top.

Sewing on snaps:

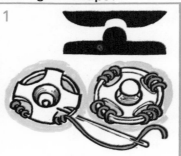

1 Choose a small needle. Sew half with knob to underside first. Make several stitches through each hole. Finish off with 3 back stitches on wrong side.

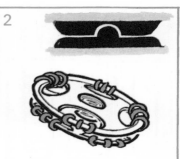

2 Be sure halves of snap are exactly opposite each other, so they fit together.

1 Rompers

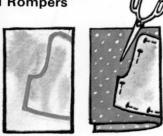

Trace pattern and cut out. Fold material lengthways. Pin pattern to material, placing fold edge against fold of material. Cut out. Repeat for second shape.

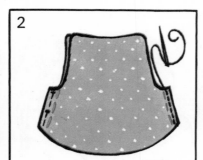

2 Remove patterns. Open out shapes. Pin, then baste together, right sides facing. Remove pins. Back stitch as shown.

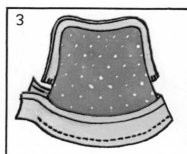

3 Turn right side out. Sew on binding around front and back of leg, neck and side edges. Turn in ends and stitch to neaten.

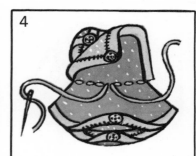

4 Make a line in running stitch around rompers with embroidery cotton Sew tassels to ends at front. Sew snaps inside shoulders and between legs.

1 Sewing on bias binding (a useful way of tidying raw edges):
Open one edge of bias binding. Lay against raw edge on right side of material. Pin, baste and sew to material along crease, with running stitch or back stitch.

2 To hold sewing steady, place over forefinger and keep in position by pressing thumb and middle finger together.

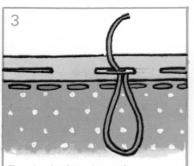

3 Turn back of sewing to face you. Bring binding forward, and baste to material above stitch line.

4 Hem neatly. Try to avoid stitches showing through on right side.

POLLY DOLLY

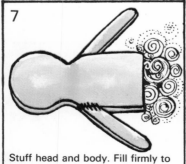

1 Trace and cut out patterns.

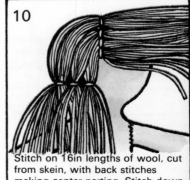

2 Pin patterns on to material and cut out 2 body shapes, 4 legs and 4 arms.

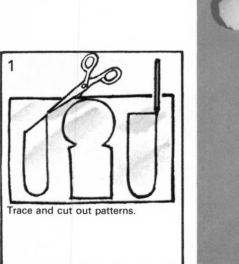

3 Right sides facing, pin and baste front of body to back, leaving openings for arms and stuffing. Remove pins, and back stitch around. Remove basting.

4 Right sides facing, pin and baste around legs and arms, leaving tops open for stuffing. Remove pins, and back stitch around. Remove basting.

5 Turn legs and arms right side out and stuff. Stitch stuffing in across top.

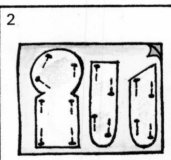

6 Snip material outside seams where shown. Turn body right side out. Pin arms into openings and stitch in all around.

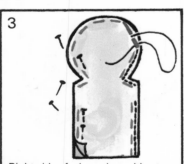

7 Stuff head and body. Fill firmly to make head and neck stiff.

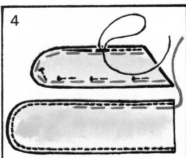

8 Turn in lower edges of body to neaten. Pin legs into body side by side. Stitch in around back and front.

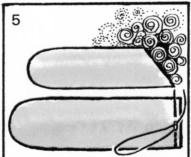

9 Trace features and cut patterns. Pin to felt, and cut out in correct colors. Stitch or glue on to face.

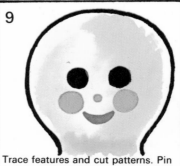

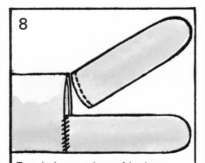

10 Stitch on 16in lengths of wool, cut from skein, with back stitches making center parting. Stitch down again—about 10 strands in each stitch—above neckline.

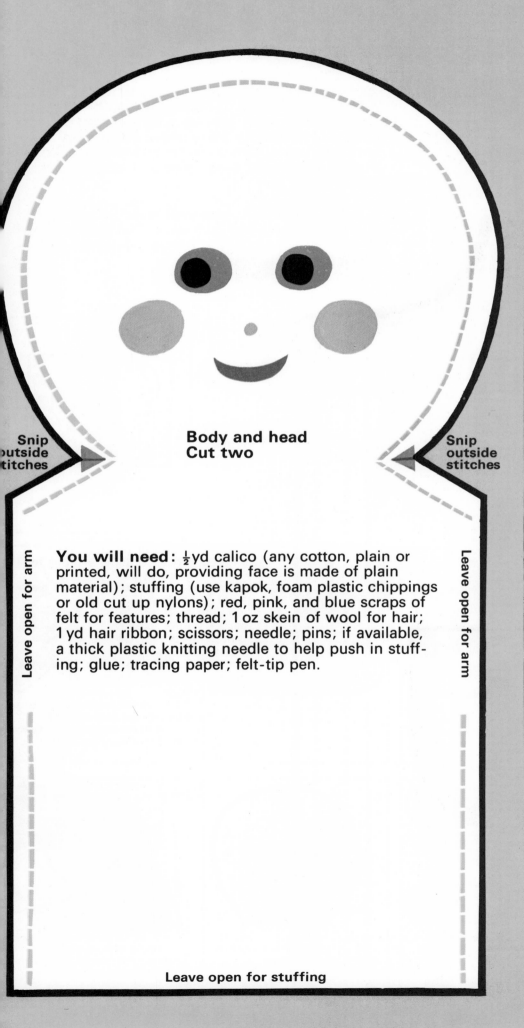

**Body and head
Cut two**

Snip outside stitches

Snip outside stitches

Leave open for arm

Leave open for arm

You will need: ½ yd calico (any cotton, plain or printed, will do, providing face is made of plain material); stuffing (use kapok, foam plastic chippings or old cut up nylons); red, pink, and blue scraps of felt for features; thread; 1 oz skein of wool for hair; 1 yd hair ribbon; scissors; needle; pins; if available, a thick plastic knitting needle to help push in stuffing; glue; tracing paper; felt-tip pen.

Leave open for stuffing

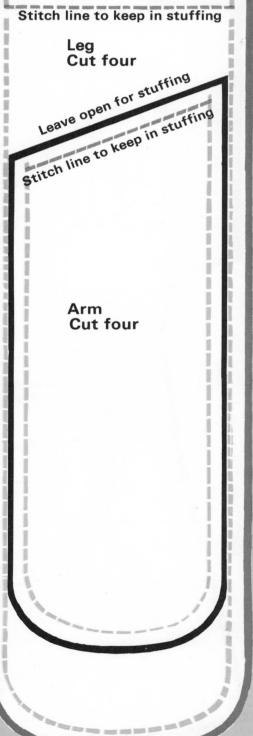

Leave open for stuffing

Stitch line to keep in stuffing

**Leg
Cut four**

Leave open for stuffing

Stitch line to keep in stuffing

**Arm
Cut four**

POLLY DOLLY'S CLOTHES

Day dress, party dress, and pants to match.

For each set of dress and pants, **you will need:** ¼yd material (cotton, wool and cotton mixture, or whipcord are good); thread; a card of bias binding; 2 snaps; ½yd lace for party dress; ½yd narrow elastic for pants; safety pin for threading elastic through waist hem; pins; needles; tracing paper; felt-tip pen.

To make each dress, **you will need:** a piece of material 9in long and 20in wide; 2yd bias binding for day dress, or 1yd bias binding, ¾yd lace and 2 snaps for party dress.

Shoulders

Neck

Bias binding

Armhole

Bias binding

Dress
Cut one front, on fold, black outline.
Cut two backs, brown outline.

Side

Front fold

First hem turning
Second hem turning

Bias binding

Pocket
Cut one
for day dress

Second hem turning

First hem turning

1 Trace and cut out one paper pattern for front around black outline, and one for back around brown outline.
2 Fold material in half, and pin front pattern against folded edge. Cut out.
3 Place remaining two pieces of material together, wrong sides facing. Pin on back pattern and cut out two shapes at once. Remove pins.
4 Right sides facing, pin, baste, then back stitch front to back shapes down sides and across shoulders.
5 Sew bias binding around neck (sew lace on first for party dress) and sleeves.
6 Make hems along lower edge, and narrow hems down edges of back opening for party dress.

Now look at opposite page where you will see how to finish off the two different styles.

To make pants for Polly Dolly, **you will need**: a piece of material 5in long and 15in wide; 14in lace ½in wide for the party dress pants, or 14in bias binding for day dress pants; 12in narrow elastic; safety pin.

1 Trace pattern, and cut out.
2 Cut material in half, to give 2 pieces, each 7½in by 5in.
3 Fold one piece in half lengthways, pin pattern against folded edge and cut out. Repeat for second shape.
4 Right sides facing, pin, baste, then back stitch front to back down sides and between legs.
5 Make hem around top leaving ½in open for elastic at side.
6 For day dress pants, sew bias binding around raw edges of legs. For party dress pants, make hems around legs, then sew lace flat on wrong side with running stitch. Join ends across and trim.
7 Pin safety pin to end of elastic, and thread through side opening of waist hem. Tie ends together, and cut ½in from knot.

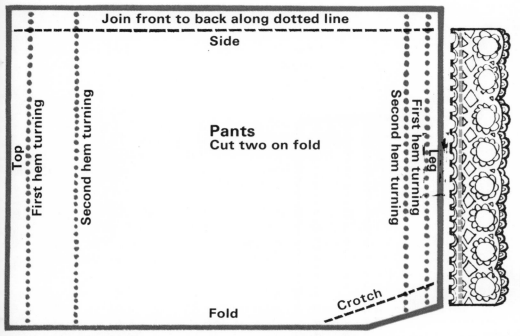

Join front to back along dotted line

Side

Top
First hem turning

Second hem turning

Pants
Cut two on fold

First hem turning
Second hem turning

Leg

Fold

Crotch

Lace for party dress pants.

1

2

1

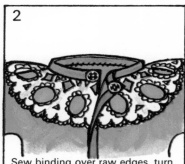

2

Day dress. Make back opening by trimming away extra hem allowance and binding edges. Fold four 6in lengths of binding in half length-ways, and stitch to neaten.

Sew strings to dress. Bind pocket and stitch on.

Party dress. Make ruffle by gathering ¾yd of lace, and stitch around neck. Turn ends under and sew to sides of back opening.

Sew binding over raw edges, turn in and stitch ends to neaten. Sew on two snaps, at top and waist.

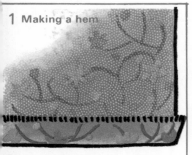

1 Making a hem

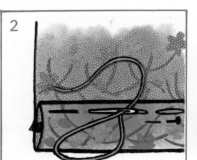

2

3

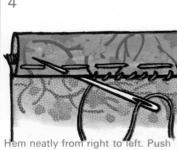

4

Turn up a short distance of raw edge on to wrong side of material, about ¼in from edge.

Turn up hem a second time to depth required, and pin in position. Repeat squares 1 and 2 until hem is completed. Then baste all around.

Remove pins. Hold material over forefinger, keeping it firm between thumb and middle finger.

Hem neatly from right to left. Push needle through to back of material below hem and up again at an angle, above and to left. Repeat. Remove basting.

Dolls' bedclothes
MATTRESS, PILLOW, SHEETS AND BLANKETS

Sheets and blankets: To make a sheet, cut a piece of cotton material 18in square, and hem around the edges.

To make a blanket, cut an 18in square of old blanket. Hem around edges, or bind with 2yd of satin ribbon 2in wide.

If you want to make a cot for your doll, turn a suitable cardboard box upside down, like a divan. Make a headboard out of cardboard. Fold a piece of printed cotton over it, turn in edges to neaten and glue on. Glue headboard to end of box. Make a frill by hemming and gathering a strip of the same material, which you could pin in position with drawing pins.

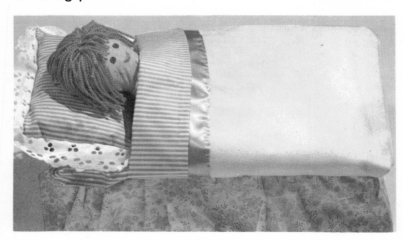

To make a mattress for Baby Billy or Polly Dolly, **you will need:** 2 pieces of cotton material, each 18in long and 12in wide; thread; kapok, foam plastic chippings, or old nylons cut up, for stuffing; scissors; pins; needle; tape measure.

To make a pillow, **you will need:** 2 pieces of cotton material, each $9\frac{1}{2}$in by $6\frac{1}{2}$in; 1 yd eyelet embroidery, $1\frac{1}{2}$in wide; kapok, foam plastic chippings or old nylons cut up, for stuffing; scissors; needle, etc.

You can vary the sizes to fit your own doll's cot, or make them smaller still to fit your dolls' house bed. Measure the bed and add a little for tucking in.

Mattress

1

Leave open

Right sides facing, pin and baste both pieces of material together around sides and one end. Remove pins, and back stitch around basting line.

2

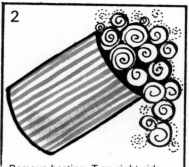

Remove basting. Turn right side out, and stuff.

3

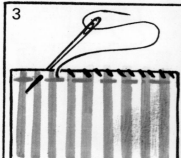

Turn in top edges, pin and baste together to close opening. Remove pins, and oversew edges together. Remove basting.

Pillow

1

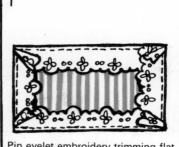

Pin eyelet embroidery trimming flat around edges of front of pillow, raw edges matching, on right side of material. Sew on close to edge with running stitch.

2

Place second pillow shape flat on top, right sides facing. Pin, baste, and back stitch together around 3 sides leaving one end open for stuffing.

3

Remove basting. Turn right side out and stuff.

4

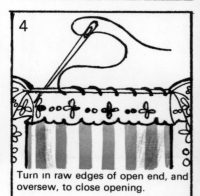

Turn in raw edges of open end, and oversew, to close opening.

PATCHWORK QUILT

People have been making beautiful patchwork quilts for hundreds of years. It is a very good way of using odd scraps of material.

You can make the squares in this doll's quilt larger or smaller, if you prefer. And you can go on adding squares until the quilt is large enough to fit your own bed. If you can persuade your friends or family to help, it will grow more quickly!

You will need: scraps of different material, each piece at least 3½in square; lining material not less than 12½in by 10in; thread; 1½yd bias binding; scissors; pins; needle; ruler; card; brown paper; felt-tip pen.

1

Paper pattern for brown paper   Patch pattern for material

To make paper pattern (stiff patch pattern), cut a card 2½in square. Make another card 3½in square for material pattern.

2

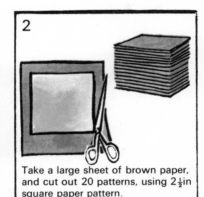

Take a large sheet of brown paper, and cut out 20 patterns, using 2½in square paper pattern.

3

Choose a selection of materials of similar thickness. Cut out 20 squares, using 3½in square card.

4

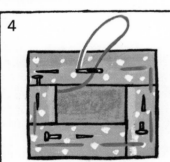

Place a brown paper square on top of a material square. Fold in sides. Pin and baste material to paper. Repeat for other squares.

5

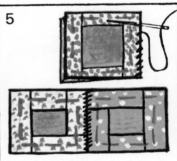

Remove pins. Place two contrasting squares together, right sides facing, and join down one side with over-sewing.

6

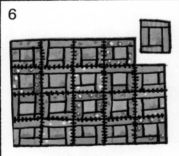

Repeat until all squares are sewn together to form a shape 5 squares long and 4 squares wide.

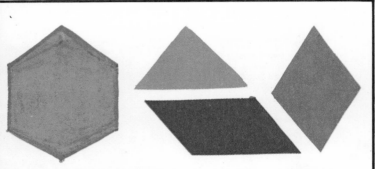

Here are some other ideas for patchwork shapes which you could use instead of squares.

7

Take out basting and paper. Press, with mother's help. Cut piece of lining material to fit. Sew around edges on to patchwork back.

8

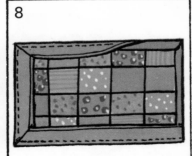

Sew bias binding all around, over lining and patchwork, to neaten edges. A patchwork quilt may be interlined and quilted, as shown on page 36.

Quilting
HEARTS-AND-FLOWERS MATS

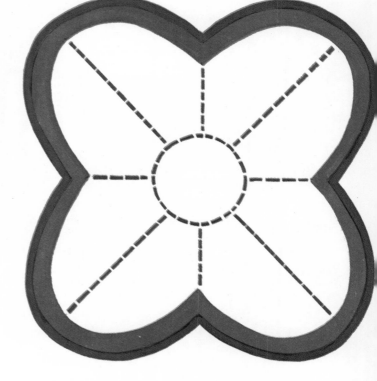

These mats will make very useful and attractive presents. You will soon see that quilting is fun to do, and not nearly as difficult as it looks.

Quilting

Top, interlining and lining are all sewn together along quilting lines. Stitches such as running stitch, back stitch or machining, may be used.

Pin and baste the shapes together, so they match exactly and lie flat.

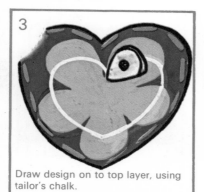

Draw design on to top layer, using tailor's chalk.

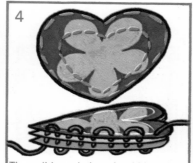

The quilting stitches should be taken through all layers of material along the chalk lines.

For each mat, **you will need**: $4\frac{1}{2}$in square of cotton material for top; same amount of blanket or flannelette for interlining; and of flannelette or cotton for lining; $\frac{1}{2}$yd bias binding; tracing paper and felt-tip pen; ruler; tailor's chalk, or chalk pencil

1 Trace and cut out patterns.
2 Pin to material, and cut out each shape in cotto interlining and lining materials.
3 Pin and baste three shapes together around edge
4 Draw quilting lines on top layer of material with chalk, and quilt along chalk lines with small, neat running stitches.
5 Pin, baste, and sew binding around edges.
6 Pleat binding at angles, and stitch to neaten.

You could make a large quilted mat 10 in wide by 7 in deep, the same way, and edge it with narrow crochet lace.

QUILTED OVEN GLOVE

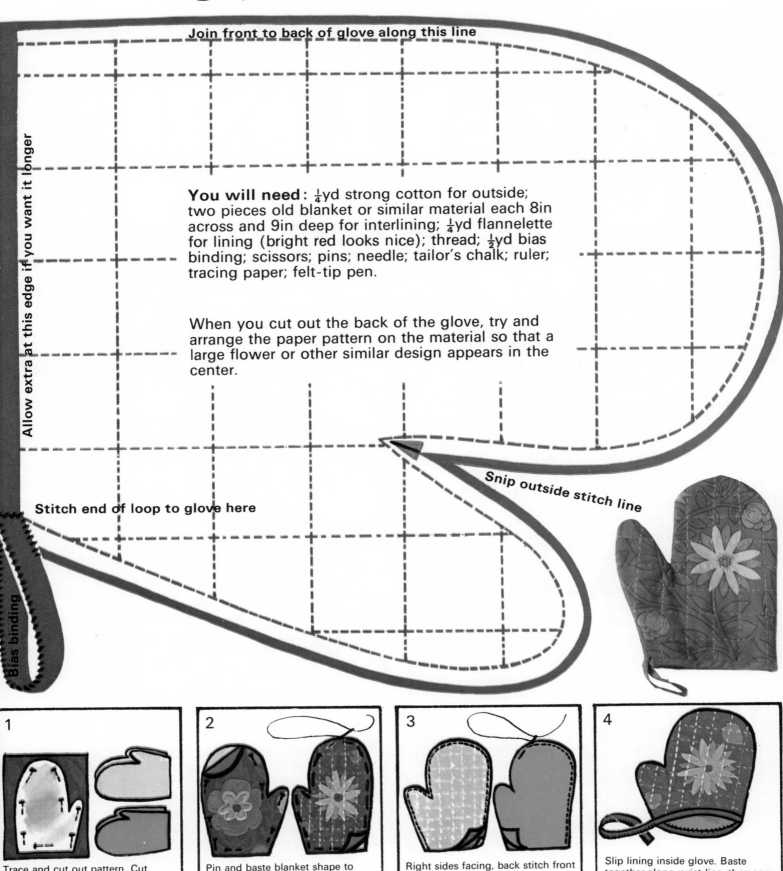

Join front to back of glove along this line

Allow extra at this edge if you want it longer

You will need : ¼yd strong cotton for outside; two pieces old blanket or similar material each 8in across and 9in deep for interlining; ¼yd flannelette for lining (bright red looks nice); thread; ½yd bias binding; scissors; pins; needle; tailor's chalk; ruler; tracing paper; felt-tip pen.

When you cut out the back of the glove, try and arrange the paper pattern on the material so that a large flower or other similar design appears in the center.

Snip outside stitch line

Stitch end of loop to glove here

Bias binding

1 Trace and cut out pattern. Cut 2 shapes each in cotton for outside, in blanket for interlining and in flannelette for lining.

2 Pin and baste blanket shape to "wrong" side of cotton shape. Repeat for other side of glove. Remove pins. Draw lines on both shapes, and quilt (2 layers only).

3 Right sides facing, back stitch front to back of glove around edges. Snip as shown. Turn right side out. Join lining shapes in same way.

4 Slip lining inside glove. Baste together along wrist line, then sew binding over raw edges, hemming down loop.

Pictures
HOUSE WITH GIANT SUNFLOWERS

Have you ever thought of making a picture by sewing? This can be done in many ways. We have chosen three: in simple cross stitch, like the alphabet on the next page; from pieces sewn on to a material background to form a collage, like our rainbow fish (p. 41); and with embroidery, using different stitches in an ornamental way.

See how neatly you can stitch this charming embroidered picture, and how quickly it will grow. You could glue it on to cardboard, or baste it along the top and bottom to strips of wood. (Allow extra canvas for this.) Or use a pretty picture frame, which would be even better.

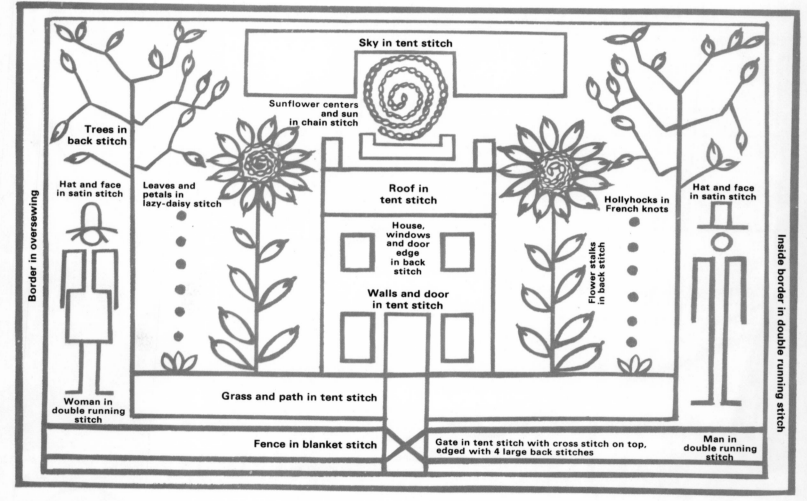

To transfer the outlines of the picture on to canvas, **you will need**: tracing paper; dressmaker's or ordinary carbon paper; felt-tip pen; ball point pen; ruler; pins; drawing pins; pencil.

1 Cut out one piece of tracing paper, and one of carbon paper, $8\frac{1}{8}$ in across by $5\frac{1}{4}$ in deep.
2 Trace all the outlines of the picture above, using felt-tip pen.
3 Place carbon paper face down on canvas, with traced picture on top. Fit together exactly, and pin at corners on to smooth piece of wood.
4 Transfer picture to canvas by drawing around outlines with ball point pen, pressing firmly, so that carbon lines are transferred to the canvas.
5 Remove tracing paper and carbon paper. If some of the lines are faint, draw them on the canvas with a pencil.

To make picture **you will need**: tapestry canvas, 8⅛ in across by 5¼ in deep; skeins of soft or stranded embroidery cotton in white, bright yellow, light and dark blue, light and dark green, light and dark brown and deep pink; scissors; tapestry needle; tracing materials; ruler.

1 Double running stitch borders. Oversew edges.
2 Back stitch house, door edge and windows, sunflower stalks and trees.
3 Chain stitch sun and sunflower centers.
4 Lazy-daisy stitch petals and leaves.
5 Blanket stitch fence.

6 Tent stitch door, gate, sky, grass, path and house.
7 Satin stitch hats and faces.
8 Double running stitch man and woman.
9 Make French knots for hollyhocks.
10 Cross stitch gate. Edge with 4 back stitches, one for each side of the square.

Other stitches used in this picture are back stitch, blanket stitch, chain stitch, cross stitch, lazy-daisy stitch, oversewing and satin stitch. If you look them up in the index at the back, you can find out where they are described in this book.

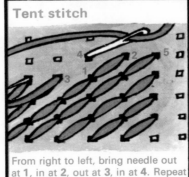

Tent stitch

From right to left, bring needle out at **1**, in at **2**, out at **3**, in at **4**. Repeat for row. Left to right, bring needle out at **2**, in at **1**, out at **5**. Repeat.

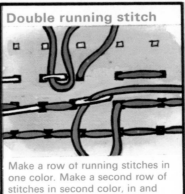

Double running stitch

Make a row of running stitches in one color. Make a second row of stitches in second color, in and out of spaces in first row.

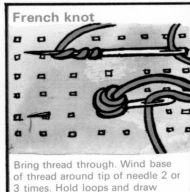

French knot

Bring thread through. Wind base of thread around tip of needle 2 or 3 times. Hold loops and draw needle through. Put in close by knot. Bring out for next knot.

CROSS STITCH ALPHABET

In the past, children used to sew cross stitch samplers in tiny stitches. Here is a modern cross stitch alphabet that would make a good present for a small child, as a picture or a mat.

To make picture **you will need**: canvas 6 holes to 1 in, 8⅜ in across by 5½ in deep; two skeins of scarlet embroidery cotton, and one of bright blue; scissors; tapestry needle.

1 Oversew edges in blue to make border.
2 Decide which method of cross stitch you would

like to use, and keep to it throughout. This will give your picture an even appearance.

3 Stitch the three lines of letters in scarlet, copying the number of crosses in each one from the picture. Leave one space of canvas between each letter, and six holes between each row. N is the odd man out, so be extra careful when you place it!

4 Work out the position of the birds, and stitch them in blue.

5 Copy the position of the double cross stitches from the picture, and stitch them in blue.

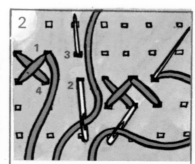
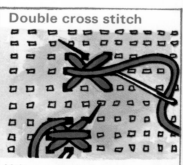

1 Cross stitch

Here is one method of cross stitch: Left to right, bring needle out at **1**, then in at **2**. Bring out at **3**. Repeat for row. Right to left, put needle in at **4**, then out at **5**. Repeat for row.

2

To make one cross at a time, bring needle out at **1**, and put it in at **2**. Bring it out at **3** and put it in at **4**. Bring needle out again at **3**. Repeat.

Double cross stitch

Make a cross stitch, but across three holes. Bring needle out center left, and in center right; out center top, in center bottom. Repeat.

RAINBOW FISH

To make this picture **you will need**: fine tapestry canvas 8¼in across by 4⅞in deep; pale green net, same size as canvas; shiny material for fish; felt scraps in yellow, orange, burnt orange, deep pink and lilac for body, and in dark blue and green for fins and eyes; thread; dark blue-green sequins; 3½in narrow lace trimming; ¾yd narrow cord or braid for frame; scissors; pins; needle; tracing paper; felt-tip pen; glue; cardboard backing.

1 Baste net background on top of canvas.
2 Trace fish around sequin outline, and cut pattern.

3 Pin pattern to shiny material, and cut out. Running stitch around edges to background.
4 Trace and cut out scales, fins and eye.
5 Sew scales to fish across top of each scale with running stitch, starting from tail, and overlapping all the way up. Edge at top with lace.
6 Sew on fins and eye with two or three stitches for each.
7 Sew sequins around edges and for mouth, using one back stitch for each sequin.
8 Edge picture with fine cord or braid, and glue on to cardboard backing.

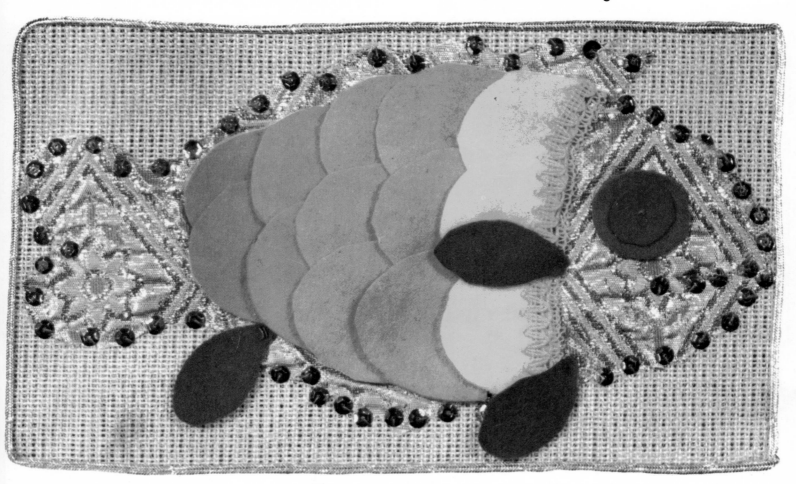

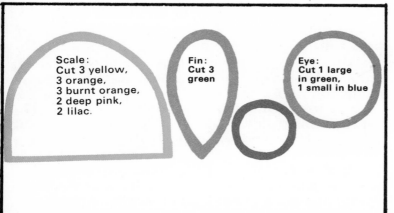

Scale:
Cut 3 yellow,
3 orange,
3 burnt orange,
2 deep pink,
2 lilac.

Fin:
Cut 3
green

Eye:
Cut 1 large
in green,
1 small in blue

This fish is made from scraps of material and brightly colored felt, cut out in shapes and stitched to backing, to form a beautiful picture edged with glittering sequins.

ALL ABOUT SEWING MACHINES

If you have been given a toy sewing machine, or can borrow a grown-up hand machine, now is the time to start using it. After a little practice, you will find that sewing by machine saves time and makes very strong seams and neat stitch lines.

But most of all, sewing by machine is exciting, because now you'll be able to tackle big, interesting jobs, such as making clothes.

Nowadays, children's toy sewing machines can be battery-driven as well as hand-operated, and work much like the simpler adults' machines. They can be expensive, however, and an old-fashioned hand machine, which can sometimes be bought at low cost, is a good alternative. It should be a make that is currently well-known and for which spare parts are available.

If the instruction booklet has been lost, you can usually obtain another, or seek advice at your sewing machine shop.

Other types of sewing machines, such as the treadle, worked by the feet, or electric powered models, are more difficult for children to use. Sophisticated electric sewing machines with high speed stitching can even be dangerous for children to operate; a grown-up should be nearby if you have been given permission to use one.

Remember to keep your fingers away from the moving machine needle, in case of accidents.

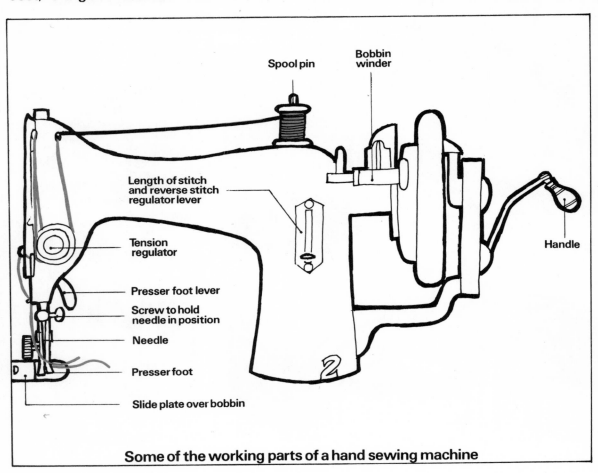

Some of the working parts of a hand sewing machine

- Spool pin
- Bobbin winder
- Length of stitch and reverse stitch regulator lever
- Tension regulator
- Presser foot lever
- Screw to hold needle in position
- Needle
- Presser foot
- Slide plate over bobbin
- Handle

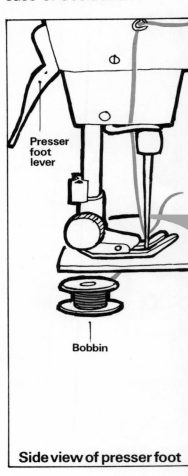

Side view of presser foot

- Presser foot lever
- Bobbin

This is a picture of a hand machine, showing the names of the parts you need to know about. You will probably notice some things that look a little different from yours, but many will be the same. The machine makes a lock stitch out of two threads. As you turn the handle, the threaded needle goes down through the material and picks up the thread from the bobbin below, making a stitch.

The material you want to stitch has to be placed on the machine under the presser foot and needle. To lift the foot, you raise the presser foot lever, a springy clip usually at the back of the machine. When the material is in position, you press this clip down, so the presser foot holds the material firm.

The needle and bobbin threads should be of equal tension, which means that one mustn't be loose and the other tight. The tension is wrong if your thread keeps breaking, or forming loops. To correct this, you could ask a grown-up to help, or refer to your instruction book.

Some toy sewing machines do not have a bobbin, and form chain stitch, which can unravel if you don't sew the last stitch down carefully by hand.

An adult's modern sewing machine can have special attachments for doing different sewing jobs. Later on, you may want to use some with the help of your instruction booklet; but for the moment, you'll find plenty of scope in straight machining.

Using a Hand Sewing Machine

When you use your machine, place it on a firm table in front of you. If necessary, put cushions on your chair so you sit at a comfortable height.

You should have a good light to work by.

Make sure, before you start, that the thickness of the needle and thread are suitable for the material you are sewing, and that you have the same thread on the bobbin as on the top. Also check that the stitch length, if it can be varied on your machine, is adjusted to give a short stitch for fine material, or a longer one for thicker material. The stitch length is altered by moving the stitch regulator.

Remember that toy sewing machines are not usually designed to sew very thick material.

Useful tips

Remove all pins from your sewing, or they might break the needle.

Your machine handle should be turned away from you, and over—like the pedals of a bicycle.

Check the evenness of the stitches on some spare material before you start.

Keep some spare empty bobbins to use when you change to thread of a different color.

Oil your machine sparingly sometimes with sewing machine oil, as shown in your instruction book. Then carefully wipe away the surplus.

1 Wind the bobbin

Pass thread under guide. Wind clockwise on to bobbin several times. Clip bobbin into winder. Press rubber wheel on to machine. Turn handle to fill evenly.

2 Thread the machine
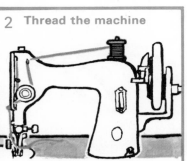
Follow instructions in booklet, or ask a grown-up to help you, or you could seek advice at a sewing machine shop.

3 Thread the needle
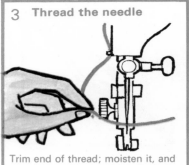
Trim end of thread; moisten it, and pass it through eye of needle from left to right. Draw thread through gently.

4 Pick up bobbin thread

Place bobbin in shuttle and draw thread around notch at side. Wind threaded needle down so it picks up bobbin thread. Draw thread up, and out to one side.

5 How to start
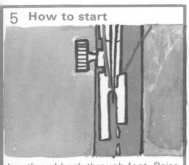
Lay thread back through foot. Raise needle and presser foot, and place sewing under. Clip presser foot lever down. Wind handle to start.

6 Keeping the stitches straight
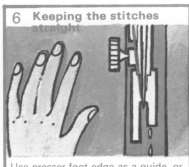
Use presser foot edge as a guide, or stitch beside basting. Guide material with your hand, but don't push or pull it. Watch out for your fingers!

7 Corners and curves
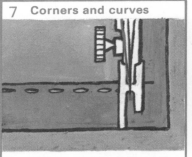
Corners: stop machine with needle down. Lift foot, turn material, then lower foot. Continue stitching. Curves: guide material around with hand.

8 How to finish off
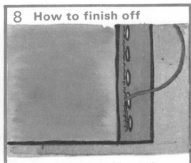
Stop close to edge with needle down. Reverse for a few stitches. Cut threads.

Beach gear
PONCHO AND HEADBAND

You will look glamorous on the beach wearing this gay toweling poncho and headband. The poncho is ideal for slipping on over your swimsuit in a chilly sea breeze, or to protect your shoulders from sunburn; and the headband will keep your hair from looking too windswept.

The poncho could also be made in woolen material, edged with a thick wool fringe.

To make poncho and headband, **you will need**: 1¼yd toweling, 36in wide (a 36in square for poncho and a strip 20in by 6in for headband); thread; 4yd fringe; short piece of elastic; scissors; needle; tape measure; pins; sewing machine, if available.

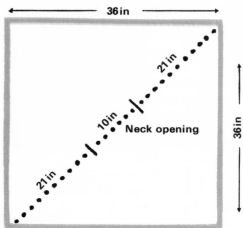

36in — Neck opening — 21in — 21in — 10in — 10in — 21in — 36in

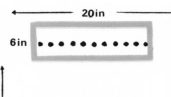

20in — 6in

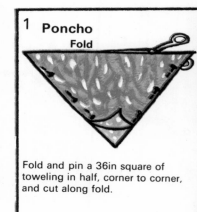

1 Poncho
Fold

Fold and pin a 36in square of toweling in half, corner to corner, and cut along fold.

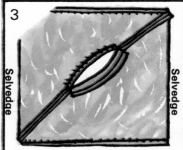

2

Right sides facing, pin and baste shoulders together where shown. Leave center open for neck. Try on for fit, then machine or back stitch along seams.

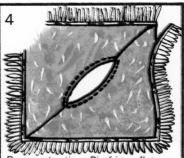

3

Selvedge · Selvedge

Pin and baste narrow hems along raw edges and around neck. Remove pins, and machine or hem. Selvedges do not need to be hemmed here.

4

Remove basting. Pin fringe flat on right side all around edges, starting at corner.

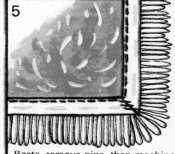

5

Baste, remove pins, then machine or back stitch all around. Sew ends of fringe over each other at corner and remove basting.

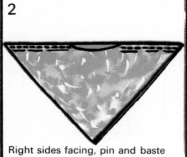

1 Headband

Cut strip of toweling 20in by 6in. Right sides facing, fold in half lengthways. Pin and baste raw edges together. Remove pins. Machine or back stitch.

2

Remove basting and turn band right side out. Cut to fit around head, leaving a gap of about 2in for elastic.

3

Turn under raw edges at ends of band. Gather and sew over ends of elastic.

BEACH BAG

If you are going for a holiday by the sea, you will be glad to avoid the struggle of trying to hold sunglasses, suntan oil, and swimming gear without dropping them. The answer is to make your own beach bag.

Greek bags like this were originally decorated with woven bands and patterns, and carried by braided and tasseled wool ropes.

Here is a simple version of these attractive bags which you can make for yourself. Choose brightly colored coarsely woven material or vivid flowered canvas to go with the white rope.

The bag is lined with plastic to make it into a real beach bag, for carrying home your damp swimsuit.

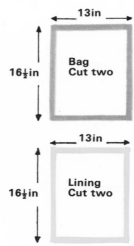

13in

16½in — Bag Cut two

13in

16½in — Lining Cut two

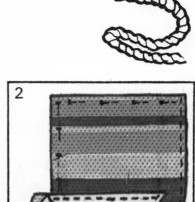

You will need: 2 pieces of furnishing heavy, open weave fabric, canvas, tapestry, or burlap, 13in wide by 16½in long; 2 pieces plastic bath curtaining material, same size; thread; 2yd thick white cotton rope; scissors; pins; needle; tape measure; ruler; paper for pattern; sewing machine, if available.

You can buy the fabric for the bag and plastic lining (½yd of each) in the furnishing department of a large store, and the rope from a haberdashery department. Try the remnants box first!

If you want to use this bag as an ordinary shoulder bag, you can make it without the lining. Or you can make a small version—11in long by 9in wide.

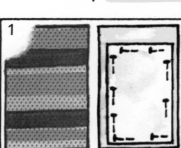

1 Measure, draw, and cut out paper pattern 13in by 16½in. Pin to fabric and cut out two bag shapes. Repeat for lining.

2 Pin a lining shape to "wrong" side of each fabric shape. Baste each pair together all around.

3 Pin sides of bag together where shown, right sides facing, then baste. Remove pins. Machine or back stitch together, leaving top open.

4 Remove basting. Turn over top all around to make 1½in hem. Baste, then machine or hem. Remove basting.

5 Turn bag right side out. Sew on rope up one side, leaving 5in spare for tassel. Try on for size, and pin to correct length.

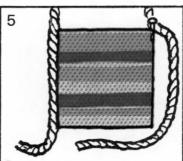

6 Oversew rope to other side of bag. Cut, leaving 5in spare at end. Knot, and fray ends for tassel. Trim ends.

Useful stowaways
PRETTY PENCIL CASE

A pencil case, shoe bag and tote bag are all useful things for school, and here we show you how to make your own. They can be pretty, like this flowered whipcord pencil case; or amusing, like the Man Friday shoe bag, that looks as if some strange little man has jumped inside it; or just plain and practical. If you stow away your belongings in their special bags, you will be able to find them at once, when you need them.

You will need: ⅛yd material (whipcord, corduroy, and suede fabric are good); thread; 8in zipper; scissors; pins; needle; pencil; ruler; paper; sewing machine, if available.

1

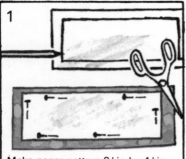

Make paper pattern 8½in by 4½in. Pin to material and cut out. Repeat for second shape.

2

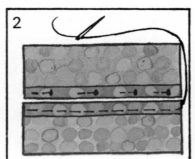

Lay shapes on table wrong sides up. Turn in edges nearest center. Pin and baste, ready to sew in zipper.

3

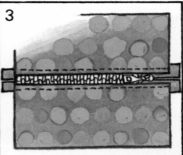

Remove pins. Turn right side up and sew in zipper. (See special instructions below.)

4

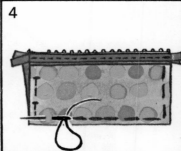

Open zipper. Fold pencil case in half, right sides facing. Pin and baste front to back down sides and along lower edge.

5

Remove pins. Machine or back stitch where basted. Hem ends of zipper to inside of case, to neaten.

6

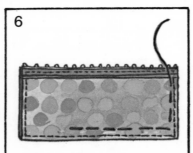

Remove basting. Turn case right side out and close zipper.

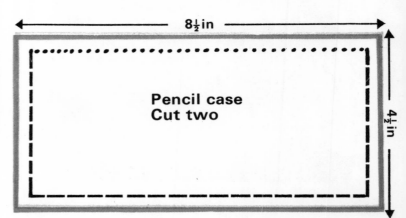

|←——————— 8½in ———————→|

Pencil case
Cut two

4½in

---

1 Sewing in a zipper

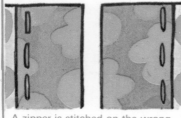

A zipper is stitched on the wrong side of the material, usually in an opening in a seam. First baste down sides of seam ⅜in from edge.

2

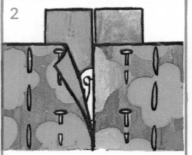

Right side up, lay sides of seams so they meet over zipper teeth, with tag at top. Allow a little space above top of zipper. Pin seams flat to zipper tapes.

3

Wrong side up, baste seams to zipper ¼in from teeth. Remove pins. Check zipper opens and shuts freely. Machine (or back stitch neatly from right side).

4

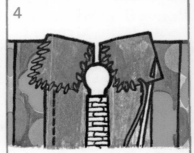

Remove all basting. Turn over both ends of tapes (at the top, diagonally), and hem to seams.

MAN FRIDAY SHOE BAG

You will need: ½yd cotton or other material—or two scraps, 12in wide by 13½in long; thread; 1yd tape; large safety pin; scraps of dark, washable material for footprints; embroidery thread; paper; pencil; scissors; pins; needle; ruler; tape measure; sewing machine, if available.

This bag is equally suitable (without the foot-prints) as a sponge bag, or brush and comb bag. Make the sponge bag in strong plastic with single turnings for hems, and the brush and comb bag in washable cotton, linen or nylon.

You could make a tote bag the same way, using two pieces of material, each 10in by 12in, and then embroider your name on it in chain stitch.

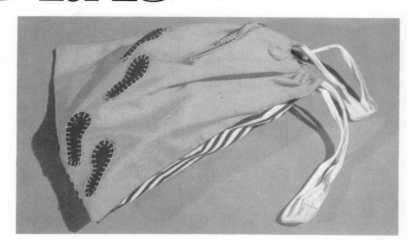

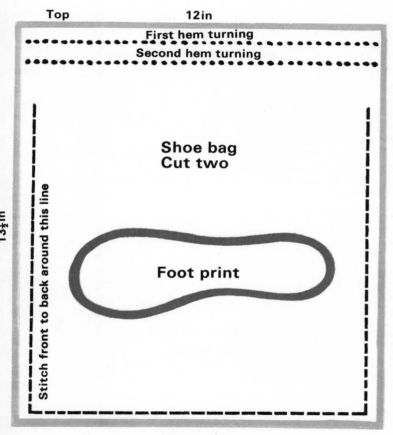

Top   12in
First hem turning
Second hem turning

13½in

Stitch front to back around this line

**Shoe bag
Cut two**

Foot print

Lower edge

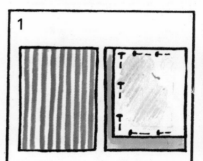

1 Measure, draw, and cut out paper pattern 12in by 13½in. Pin to material and cut out. Repeat for second shape.

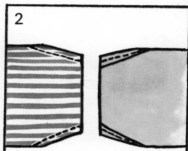

2 Pin and baste narrow hems, tapering as shown, for 2½in down sides from top. Remove pins. Machine or hem.

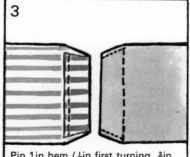

3 Pin 1in hem (¼in first turning, ¾in second turning), across top. Baste. Remove pins, then machine or hem.

4 Right sides facing, pin front to back around sides and lower edge. Baste together. Remove pins. Machine or back stitch where basted.

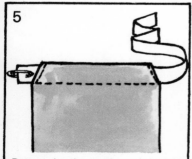

5 Remove basting, and turn bag right side out. Pin safety pin through end of tape, and thread through hem, all around top.

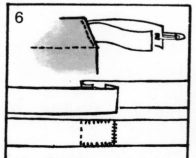

6 Allow 6in extra at each end of tape, and cut. Turn in ends, and place over each other. Stitch together all around.

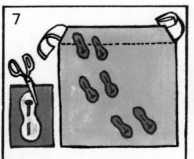

7 Trace and cut out footprint pattern. Cut out several footprints in suitable material, and pin to one side of bag.

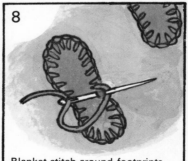

8 Blanket stitch around footprints to sew them to bag.

PURSE BELT

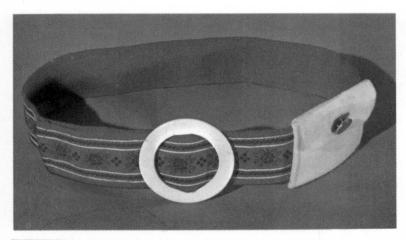

You will need: 1yd plain carpet braid, $1\frac{1}{2}$in wide; 1yd embroidered ribbon, or daisy lace, if you prefer; a buckle without a prong; felt for purse, 5in by 3in; threads; gilt button; snap; scissors; pins; needles; small piece of cardboard; tracing paper; felt-tip pen; sewing machine, if available.

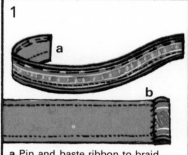

1
a Pin and baste ribbon to braid. Remove pins, and machine along both edges. **b** Hem one end, then remove basting.

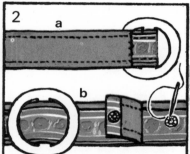

2
a Slot belt through buckle, turn end back and hem down. **b** Sew snap to hold loose end of belt in position, to fit.

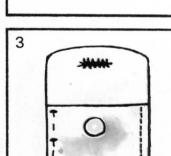

3
Make purse pattern, and cut one in felt. Fold up, pin, and back stitch down sides. Sew on button. Fold flap over; cut buttonhole. Edge with buttonhole stitch.

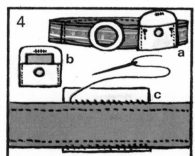

4
a Pin purse to belt. **b** Slip small cardboard inside purse, so that when you stitch belt to purse (**c**) you stitch to back only. Remove cardboard.

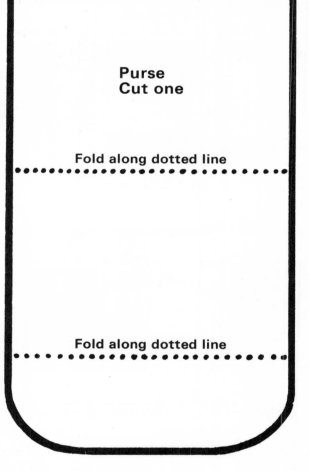

Purse
Cut one

Fold along dotted line

· · · · · · · · · · · · · · · · · · · ·

Fold along dotted line

· · · · · · · · · · · · · · · · · · · ·

You can make the purse separately, if you like.

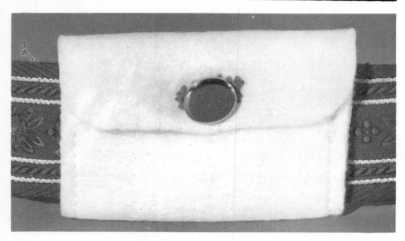

SHOULDER BAG

You will need: ¼yd woolen material, whipcord or corduroy, or a piece of material 16in wide by 7½in long; same amount taffeta or cotton for lining; thread; 1yd plain carpet braid, 1in wide; button—or 7in zipper; ¼yd fringe; scissors; pins; needle; ruler; pencil; paper for pattern.

Bag Cut two

Lining Cut two

← 8in →

1

Draw and cut out paper pattern. Pin to bag material and cut out two shapes. Repeat for lining.

2

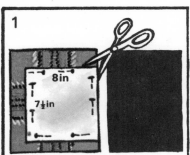

Pin and baste a lining shape to wrong side of each bag shape. Remove pins.

3

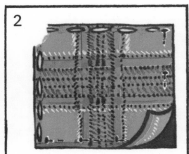

Right sides facing, pin and baste front to back of bag. Remove pins and join by machine or back stitch around 3 sides. Remove basting.

4

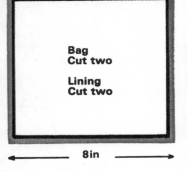

Turn over top edges to make 1in hem. Machine or hem by hand. If you want a zipper instead of a button, turn hem once, and see page 46.

5

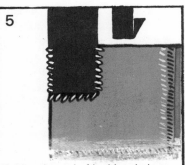

Fold under end of braid and pin to bag at left. Hem to bag down sides and across lower edge.

6

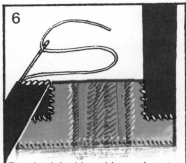

Turn back braid, and hem where top of bag meets front of braid. Fit and pin other end of strap, and stitch the same way.

7

Sew button to inside of bag hem, and make buttonhole in front hem. Sew fringe to front of bag with running stitch.

---

1 Sewing on a button

Place button. Push needle up through 1st hole, across and down through 2nd. Repeat for 3rd and 4th. Allow about ⅛in shank. Repeat 3 times.

2

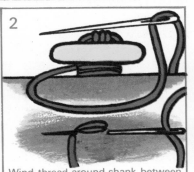

Wind thread around shank between button and material, and finish off with 3 back stitches on the wrong side.

1 Making a buttonhole

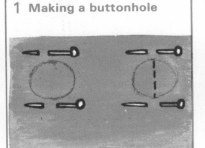

Place material over button and mark position of buttonhole with pins. Allow extra at each side. Mark line with running stitches or pencil line.

2

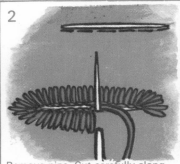

Remove pins. Cut carefully along line—if 2 layers of material, through both. Sew down sides with very close blanket stitches. Oversew around ends.

Clothes for you
ALL ABOUT MATERIAL

It is fun to make your own clothes. You can choose the exact design, material and color that you want, and the trimmings you like best. And clothes which you make yourself usually cost less, so you can often have something new to wear.

We have designed some attractive clothes here especially for you to make, such as a Tyrolean style dirndl skirt and headscarf, a fashionable jerkin or vest, and other things besides.

All the patterns have been carefully designed to adapt to fit average size girls aged seven to twelve years. With the help of the measuring list opposite you can cut them out smaller or larger, so they will fit you perfectly when made up.

To do this, compare your measurements with the pattern we have given, and draw the pattern shape to your correct size on the tracing paper. Do remember to allow extra for hems and seams. Then fit the patterns on you, pinned together, for a final check before you cut out your material.

Be careful to put the pins through the material at the neck, or under the arms, with the points away from your body, to avoid pricking yourself.

By the way, if you have to cut out the garment much larger than the pattern we have given, don't forget to buy extra material.

You will find it helpful if you press the sewing at each stage—and when it is finished, so that the completed garment can be seen in all its glory.

Shopping for material
Before you go to the shops, make a list of all the things you are going to need for the pattern you've chosen, including material, thread, bias binding, snaps, and so on.

To begin with you'll want to buy material. It's a good idea to look on the remnants counter first. Remnants are ends of rolls of material that are sold off cheaply, and are often long enough to make clothes for you.

Important questions to ask about material you would like to buy are: Will it stretch, crease or fray? Will it wear well? Is it drip dry? Does it have to be dry cleaned? Is it difficult to sew?

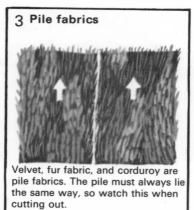

Shopping list
1 yd. red polka-dotted cotton
1 reel red thread
1 yd. narrow elastic
1½ yds. embroidered ribbon
1½ yds. ric-rac braid
1 pkt. needles
dog biscuits

How to choose material
There are so many different kinds of material, you may wonder how to choose the right one for what you plan to make. At present it is sold by the yard or part of a yard, and you will notice it is usually 36 in wide for lighter weight material. Heavy fabric is usually 54 in wide so you will need less of it. The assistant should be able to advise you on the different amounts you will need to buy.

Summer clothes are best made of cotton, or man-made fibers such as dacron, nylon, or a mixture of these fibers. Remember that transparent materials will need to be lined.

For cool days, cotton whipcord, brushed rayon, or a wool and cotton mixture are all suitable materials. They are easy to sew, moderately priced and generally wash well.

For winter clothes choose heavy corduroy, woolen material, or bulky man-made materials such as orlon. Fur fabric or velvet are good, but expensive. Rough or loosely woven materials are best lined.

Ask if the material will wash. It would be so disappointing to make it up and find it shrank or the colors ran, or you found yourself unexpectedly having to pay dry cleaner's bills after wearing it.

You will need thread to sew your material; match it, or choose a slightly darker shade of the same color, so it won't show.

---

1 Woven material

This is straightforward to sew, but when loosely woven it may fray. Oversew raw seam edges.

2 Knitted material

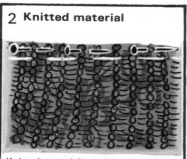

Knitted material tends to stretch. Pin and baste it extra carefully to keep seams perfectly matched and adjust stitch so material does not pucker.

3 Pile fabrics

Velvet, fur fabric, and corduroy are pile fabrics. The pile must always lie the same way, so watch this when cutting out.

4 Needles

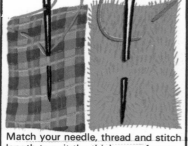

Match your needle, thread and stitch length to suit the thickness of your material.

MEASURING AND CUTTING OUT

Patterns are made different front and back to fit your own shape, so you can move easily in the clothes made up from them. Extra is allowed for gathering, seams, hems, pleats and darts if they are included.

To check if your pattern fits, you should know your measurements. Hold the tape around or against you, firmly but not tightly. Write the measurements in a notebook, or in this book.

Measuring list for garments in this book
1 Back length from neck to waist:
   Measure from knobby bone in back of neck to center back.
2 Back length from waist to hem:
   Measure from center back to hem edge.
3 Back length from neck to hem:
   Measure from knobby bone in back of neck to hem edge.
4 Front length from neck to waist:
   Measure from neck hollow to waist.
5 Front length from waist to hem:
   Measure from waist to hem edge.
6 Front length from neck to hem:
   Measure from neck hollow to hem edge.
7 Chest:
   Hold tape level around widest part of chest.
8 Waist:
   Hold tape around waist.
9 Hips:
   Hold tape around widest point of hips.

Cutting out your clothes
Material is often folded in half lengthways when you buy it. There is a woven edge each side, called a selvedge. If you have to cut out a pattern on folded material, it isn't just a question of placing the pattern along the folded edge of material as it is folded when you buy it; this way you would be left with a lot of wasted material at the sides. You should refold your material carefully to the width of the pattern, keeping the selvedges parallel. Lay your pattern flat on the material, and pin it every few inches around the edges, to keep it in place.

Cutting out a pattern

1 Get your scissors, pins and pattern ready. Lay your material flat on table, opened out with selvedges at sides.

2 Always place pattern with straight of fabric line matching straight of fabric parallel to selvedges.

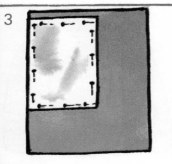

3 For a single shape not requiring folded material, place pattern close to selvedge and raw edge of material.

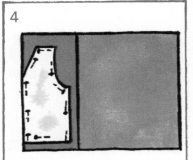

4 To cut pattern on fold, economically, refold material lengthways, right sides out, so it is just wider than pattern when folded.

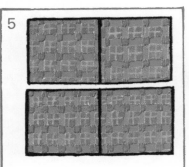

5 Plaid or stripes should match at the seams. Cut out first shape, then place second shape to match at seam before cutting out.

6 Work flat on table. Cut out roughly close to pattern, then carefully around pattern, using long careful cuts with scissors.

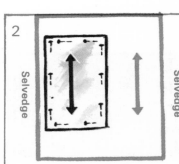

DIRNDL SKIRT

A simple gathered skirt with elastic around the waist is one of the easiest garments to make. To vary it, you could use different material such as tartan or velvet, with or without braid trimming. Or you could add a deep frill of the same material around the hem.

Before you begin, take your measuring notebook and head one of its pages "Skirt". Decide what length from the waist you want your skirt to be. Perhaps a grown-up would help you by holding the tape measure. Add 3in for hems, and write down the total. Draw your pattern to this length.

The skirt measurements given on this page will fit most girls from about 8 to 11 years old.

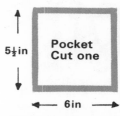

Pocket Cut one
5½in
6in

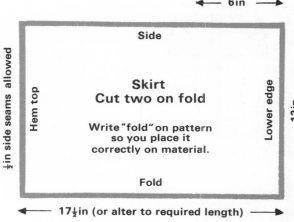

Side

Hem top

Skirt Cut two on fold

Write "fold" on pattern so you place it correctly on material.

Lower edge

½in side seams allowed

12in

Fold

17½in (or alter to required length)

1

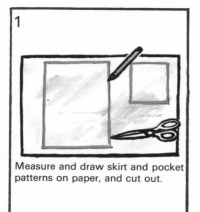

Measure and draw skirt and pocket patterns on paper, and cut out.

2

Fold of material

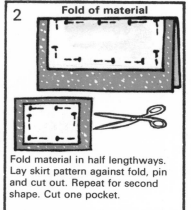

Fold material in half lengthways. Lay skirt pattern against fold, pin and cut out. Repeat for second shape. Cut one pocket.

3

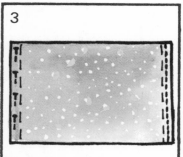

Remove pins. Open out skirt shapes and place together, right sides facing. Pin and baste together down sides. Remove pins, and machine or back stitch.

4

Turn a hem at the top—¼in first, ¾in second. Pin and baste. Remove pins. Then machine or hem.

5

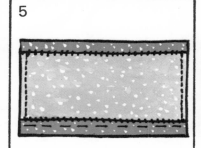

Make a hem at the lower edge—¼in first, 1¾in second. Pin and baste. Remove pins. Then machine or hem.

6

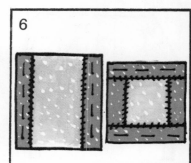

To make pocket, turn narrow hems down sides, then along top and lower edge, on to wrong side of material.

7

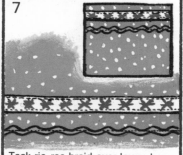
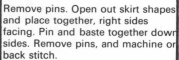

Tack ric-rac braid over lower hem of skirt. Sew ribbon on flat, 1in above braid. Trim pocket similarly, along top hem.

8

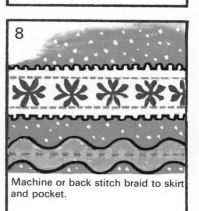

Machine or back stitch braid to skirt and pocket.

9

Pin and baste pocket to front of skirt 3½in from top edge, and 2in from side seam. Remove pins, then machine or back stitch. Remove basting.

10

Make buttonhole inside waist hem, and thread elastic through. Adjust for size, pin, cut elastic, and hem ends over each other.

HEADSCARF

For skirt and headscarf, **you will need**: 1 3/8 yd cotton or other material 36 in wide; thread; 2 1/2 yd each of embroidered ribbon and ric-rac braid; 1 yd ribbon, 1/2 or 3/4 in wide, to match material; 3/4 yd lace trimming for headscarf; 1 yd elastic, and large-eyed blunt needle or safety pin for threading it through waist hem; paper, pencil and tape measure or ruler to make paper pattern.

For the skirt, **you will need**: 1 yd material; 2 yd braid; 2 yd ribbon.

For the headscarf, **you will need**: 12 in square of material; 1/2 yd ric-rac braid; 1/2 yd embroidered ribbon, 1/2 or 3/4 in wide, to match material; 3/4 yd lace trimming, 3/4 in wide.

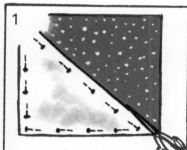

1 Draw 12 in square of paper for pattern. Fold in half corner to corner, diagonally, and cut in two. Pin one triangle to material and cut one headscarf shape.

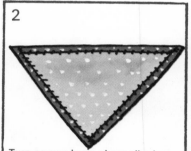

2 Turn narrow hems along all edges. Ends of hems should be turned in and stitched, to neaten.

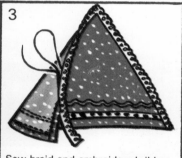

3 Sew braid and embroidered ribbon across headscarf as on skirt. Sew lace down each side, underneath back edges of hems.

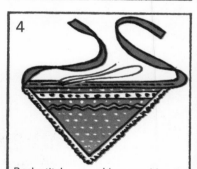

4 Back stitch or machine matching ribbon on top of front edge of headscarf, leaving long ends to tie under chin.

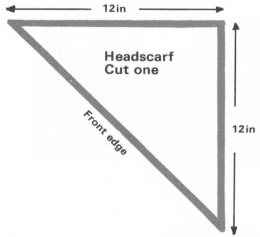

12 in

Headscarf Cut one

Front edge

12 in

APRON

Wear this apron when you are cooking or painting, or doing any messy jobs, and you will look both smart and sensible. If you want to make it larger or smaller, check your measurements in your notebook, and adjust your pattern accordingly.

To make the apron, **you will need**: ½yd strong cotton, or other suitable material; thread; 2yd colored braid or tape, 1in wide, for the halter and tie strings; scissors; pins; needles; sewing machine if available.

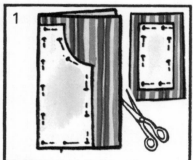

1 Fold material in half lengthways. Place and pin pattern against fold, and cut out apron shape. Cut out pocket—across stripes, if striped material.

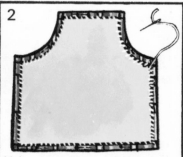

2 Make narrow hems around apron. Hem curved edges first, then sides, then top and lower edges. Strong cotton only needs a single turning for hems when machined.

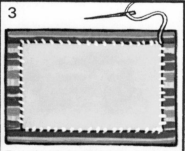

3 To make pocket, first hem down sides, then across top and lower edges.

4 Place pocket on apron 7¼in from top and about 3¼in from side. Pin, baste, then machine or back stitch to apron, leaving top open.

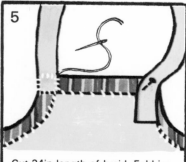

5 Cut 24in length of braid. Fold in one end, pin under corner at top and machine or hem on all around. Try on for size, cut, fold and sew other end to apron.

6 Cut 2 lengths of braid, each 24in long. Turn in one end of each, and machine or hem to sides of apron.

To make pattern for apron, **you will need**: tracing paper; ruler; tape measure; felt-tip pen; scissors.

1 Cut a piece of tracing paper $9\frac{1}{8}$in wide and $17\frac{1}{2}$in long, or to required length, and write "Top" along one short edge.
2 Place the paper across these two pages with the end marked "Top" placed against the line marked "Top".
3 Trace the curved line on to the paper, and cut along it.
4 Write "Fold" along long straight side.

To make pocket pattern, measure and cut out a piece of paper 11in wide and 7in deep.

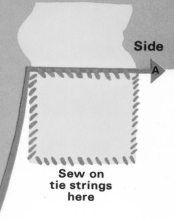

Side

A

Sew on tie strings here

Curve down side of chest

Sew on neck halter here

**Apron
Cut one on fold**

Top

Fold

**Extend green lines at A and B
another $9\frac{1}{2}$in or more,
and draw line across to join ends.
This completes the apron pattern.**

B

JERKIN AND VEST

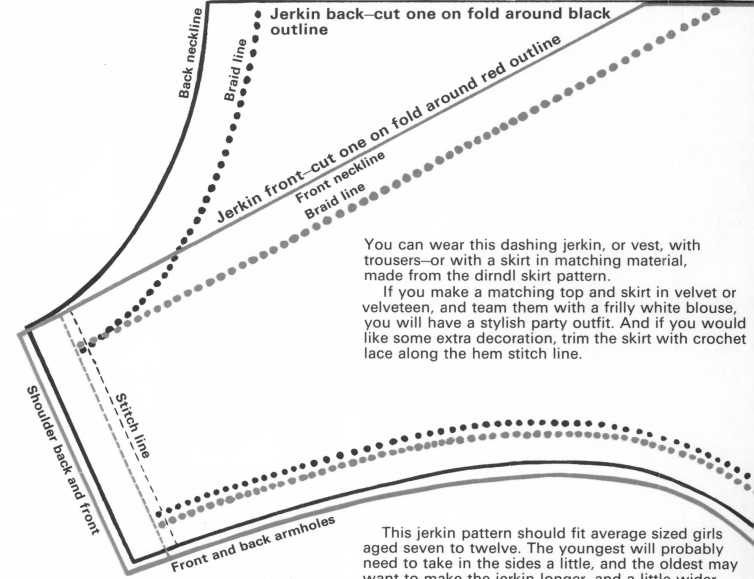

Back neckline

Braid line

Jerkin back—cut one on fold around black outline

Jerkin front—cut one on fold around red outline

Front neckline

Braid line

Shoulder back and front

Stitch line

Front and back armholes

You can wear this dashing jerkin, or vest, with trousers—or with a skirt in matching material, made from the dirndl skirt pattern.

If you make a matching top and skirt in velvet or velveteen, and team them with a frilly white blouse, you will have a stylish party outfit. And if you would like some extra decoration, trim the skirt with crochet lace along the hem stitch line.

This jerkin pattern should fit average sized girls aged seven to twelve. The youngest will probably need to take in the sides a little, and the oldest may want to make the jerkin longer, and a little wider. Check in your notebook for your correct measurements, and compare them with the pattern size.

To sew on doubled over braid, slip raw edge of material inside folded braid. Then pin, baste, and machine or back stitch through all layers.

To make jerkin

1
Trace patterns separately on folded paper—front around red outline and back around black outline. Unfold and pin together. Try on and adjust to fit.

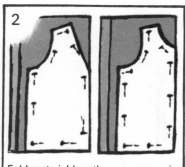

2
Fold material lengthways economically. Refold patterns, pin against fold, and cut out one front and one back.

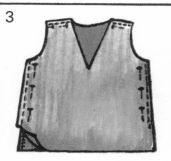

3
Right sides facing, pin front to back along shoulders and down sides. Leave side slits open. Machine or back stitch seams. Hem sides of slits.

4
Right side out, edge neck, armholes and lower edges of front and back with braid or binding. Pleat braid in point of neck; turn in ends, and hem to neaten.

To make jerkin, or vest, **you will need**: 1yd material 36in wide (corduroy, whipcord, woolen material or heavy cotton are good. Allow extra if your pattern is larger); thread; 3yd braid or bias binding for the jerkin, and $3\frac{3}{4}$yd braid or bias binding for the vest (doubled over braid is best); scissors; pins; needle; tape measure; paper for pattern; felt-tip pen; ruler; sewing machine, if available.

To make vest, start by cutting out patterns as for jerkin. Then:

Straight of fabric

1 Cut down center fold of front pattern, making two halves. You may like to cut the lower inside corners to make them curved.

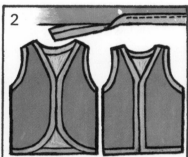

2 Make up vest as jerkin but without slits. Sew braid or bias binding around all edges.

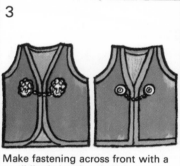

3 Make fastening across front with a small lion's head and chain, or any other decorative fastening.

Braid line

Lower edge front and back—lengthen here if required

Stitch line

Side front and back—make wider or narrower here

Slit

SNOWBALL WINTER HOOD

We have called this a "Snowball Hood" because it is as white and soft as snow, and because it is just the right thing to wear in winter when you go tobogganing or sliding on the ice.

You can make a lovely ball for a baby by making a larger pompon, using different colored wools. The instructions for making one are on the opposite page.

To make hood and scarf, **you will need**: ½yd brushed orlon in white (or a color, if you prefer); thread; 1 skein embroidery cotton in blue; scissors; pins; needles; paper for pattern; ruler; felt-tip pen; sewing machine. (You may hand sew if you prefer.)

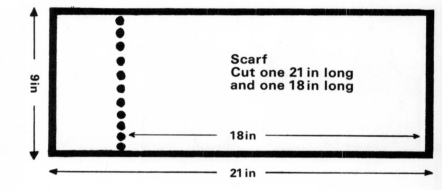

Fold

Hood
Cut one on fold
10½ in by 9 in

Back

9 in

Lower edge

10½ in

Scarf
Cut one 21 in long
and one 18 in long

9 in

18 in

21 in

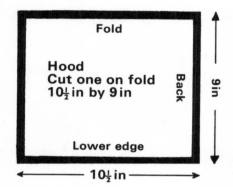

1 Draw and cut out paper patterns. Pin patterns to material, and cut out hood and scarf. Make 1½ in hem along front of hood.

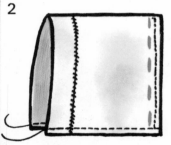

2 Right sides facing, fold hood in half so 10½in edges match. Join hood down back. Baste and try for size. Machine or back stitch seam. Stitch gathering thread.

3 Right sides facing, pin, baste, then machine or back stitch pieces for scarf together at one end.

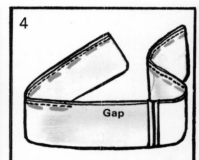

4 Fold scarf in half lengthways, matching center seams. Leave 15in gap at center. Pin, baste and machine sides together. Turn right side out through center gap.

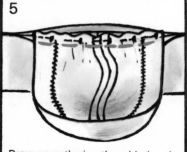

5 Draw up gathering thread in hood, try for fit, and fix around pin. Pin hood, right sides facing, to one side of gap in scarf, center seams matching. Machine together.

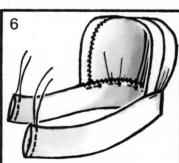

6 Turn in open edge of scarf to neaten. Pin inside hood above gathering line. Hem to hood. Turn in ends of scarf. Run gathering threads around ends.

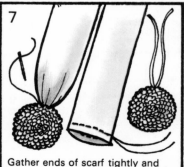

7 Gather ends of scarf tightly and secure with 2 or 3 back stitches. Make two pompons and sew to ends.

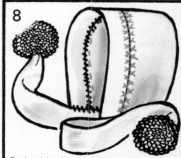

8 Embroider herringbone stitch along stitch line of hem.

Herringbone stitch

Herringbone stitch, which is fun to do, is good for making flat borders in embroidery, and is used sometimes for sewing on appliqué designs. Apart from looking pretty, it is also used for sewing down a hem on thick material. If you are making a garment, or something in bulky cloth, it would be difficult to turn over the edge twice for the hem. You should make a single turning only, then pin and baste down the raw edge, and sew it flat to the material using neat herringbone. This is also the stitch to use when sewing a mending patch into thick material.

There are several ways of making herringbone stitch, but this is the most common.

To make pompon **you will need**: a piece of thin, stiff cardboard; pair of compasses, or circular objects you can draw around; ruler; pencil; skein of white wool (or matching color); large needle; a pair of medium sized, sharp-pointed scissors.

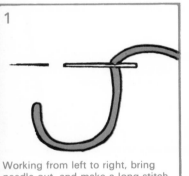

1

Working from left to right, bring needle out, and make a long stitch above to right. Bring needle out a short stitch to left.

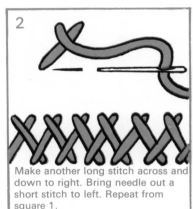

2

Make another long stitch across and down to right. Bring needle out a short stitch to left. Repeat from square 1.

1 Making a pompon

Draw 2 circles on cardboard using same center—one ¾in across, one 2¼in across—and cut around lines. Repeat for 2nd ring.

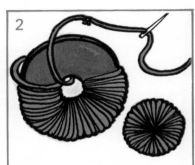

2

Match cardboard rings together, and wind wool around and around through hole until filled. Join lengths of wool as you go by tying ends.

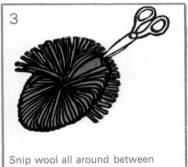

3

Snip wool all around between cardboard rings.

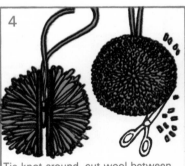

4

Tie knot around, cut wool between cardboard rings, then carefully snip away cardboard. Trim pompon until smooth and even.

LION SLIPPERS

Felt lining
Cut two in blue

You will need: a pair of cork soles in your size; 9 in square of blue felt; 9 in square of light orange felt; 12 in square of yellow felt; strip of orange felt, 11 in long and ¾ in wide, for fringe; scraps of black and white felt for eyes and nose; scraps of black and white embroidery cotton; scissors; pins; darning or embroidery needle; thimble to fit your middle finger; ruler; tailor's chalk.

To make each sole:

1. Draw around cork sole on to blue felt, and cut out shape.
2. Put thimble on middle finger of your sewing hand, and sew felt shape to top of sole in blanket stitch. Leave openings at each side, so that yellow top can be inserted later.

Your toes will be his teeth!

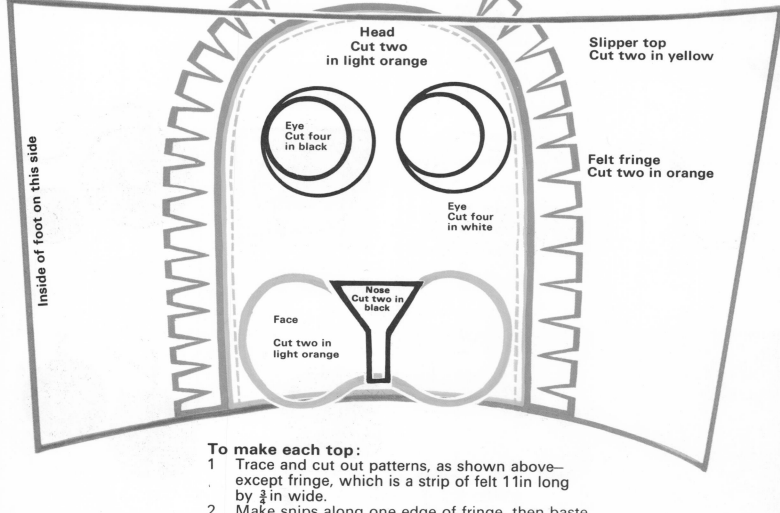

Inside of foot on this side

Head
Cut two
in light orange

Slipper top
Cut two in yellow

Eye
Cut four
in black

Eye
Cut four
in white

Felt fringe
Cut two in orange

Nose
Cut two in black

Face
Cut two in light orange

To make each top:

1. Trace and cut out patterns, as shown above—except fringe, which is a strip of felt 11 in long by ¾ in wide.
2. Make snips along one edge of fringe, then baste around top and sides of head.
3. Baste fringed top to yellow top, as shown on pattern.
4. Back stitch head and fringe to top, using orange cotton.
5. Back stitch face to head down center, using orange cotton.
6. Sew eyes to head—first whites, then black pupils—using back stitches through centers. Sew on black nose with back stitches across top and down center.
7. Make some orange whiskers out of embroidery cotton, and sew on.
8. Place foot on sole. Tuck top over foot and into gaps at sides between felt and sole, making sure it fits closely. Wearing thimble, oversew top to sole along sides.

INDEX

Here is an alphabetical list of stitches and special sewing jobs.
There is a page number beside each item,
with an illustration to help you find what you are looking for.
When you turn to the page you want, you will find one or more
blue squares which will show you, by instructions and pictures,
exactly what you want to know.